D0285457

To:

Al Hampton

From:

Dave Stuck    ERS

Date:

6/22/15

# GOD'S
## WISDOM
### for Your Life

# Men's Edition

BARBOUR
PUBLISHING

Published by Barbour Publishing, Inc., P.O. Box 719, Uhrichsville, Ohio 44683, www.barbourbooks.com

*Our mission is to publish and distribute inspirational products offering exceptional value and biblical encouragement to the masses.*

Printed in the United States of America.

# Contents

## Introduction

When men have questions, God has answers!

*God's Wisdom for Your Life: Men's Edition* is a compilation of more than 1,000 Bible verses, categorized under 70 key life topics. Drawing from varied Bible translations for ease of reading, this book features subjects such as Brothers, Competitiveness, Emotions, Exercise, Fatherhood, Leadership, Legacy, Lust, Mentoring, Service, Sports, and Temptation.

Each category is accompanied by a contemporary "life application" introduction, while quotations, prayers, and brief devotional thoughts are also scattered throughout—making *God's Wisdom for Your Life: Men's Edition* your one-stop resource for encouragement, challenge, and hope.

■ ■ ■

# I

*Abiding*

Abide is a word rich in meaning—and without exploring these meanings we will never fully understand what Jesus means when He says, "If you abide in Me, and My words abide in you," and when He commands, "Abide in My love" (John 15:7, 9 NKJV).

The original Greek word means "to remain, to continue"—so we are to remain in Christ and allow His words to remain in us.

This is not a static thing. To continue means to "keep on" being faithful to Him, to make up our minds to be near Jesus on an ongoing basis.

Our English word *abide* also means "to stick or adhere to" something, as in the expression "abide by the rules."

Perhaps the deepest meaning of abide is "to dwell, to live in." So we are to dwell in Christ and allow His words to have their home in us.

Abide in Me, and I in you. As the branch cannot bear fruit of itself, unless it abides in the vine, neither can you, unless you abide in Me. I am the vine, you are the branches. He who abides in Me, and I in him, bears much fruit; for without Me you can do nothing.
JOHN 15:4–5 NKJV

> *The branch of the vine does not worry, and toil, and rush here to seek for sunshine, and there to find rain. No; it rests in union and communion with the vine; and at the right time, and in the right way, is the right fruit found on it. Let us so abide in the Lord Jesus.*
> HUDSON TAYLOR

He who dwells in the shelter of the Most High will abide in the shadow of the Almighty.
PSALM 91:1 NASB

They that trust in the L**ORD** shall be as mount Zion, which cannot be removed, but abideth for ever.
PSALM 125:1 KJV

And I will pray the Father, and he shall give you another Comforter, that he may abide with you for ever.
JOHN 14:16 KJV

*Abiding in God changes our relationship with our fellow humans. We cannot keep our heads in the clouds as we walk with Jesus on earth. We must deal day by day with others and through our actions show them the love we have received.*

He that loveth his brother abideth in the light, and there is none occasion of stumbling in him.
1 JOHN 2:10 KJV

Whosoever abideth in him sinneth not: whosoever sinneth hath not seen him, neither known him.
1 JOHN 3:6 KJV

As the Father loved Me, I also have loved you; abide in My love. If you keep My commandments, you will abide in My love, just as I have kept My Father's commandments and abide in His love.
JOHN 15:9–10 NKJV

I have come as a light into the world, that whoever believes in Me should not abide in darkness.
JOHN 12:46 NKJV

*Abiding is an active service of trust in God that demands much of us but also provides us with untold blessings.*

If you abide in Me, and My words abide in you, you will ask what you desire, and it shall be done for you. By this My Father is glorified, that you bear much fruit; so you will be My disciples.
JOHN 15:7–8 NKJV

He that saith he abideth in him ought himself also so to walk, even as he walked.
1 JOHN 2:6 KJV

Now he who keeps His commandments abides in Him, and He in him. And by this we know that He abides in us, by the Spirit whom He has given us.
1 JOHN 3:24 NKJV

*To abide with Christ—to stay with Him and to learn from Him— is to continually receive eyes to see, ears to hear, and a heart to obey.*
ANGELA MCGUFFEY

Anyone who hates a brother or sister is a murderer, and you know that no murderer has eternal life residing in him.
1 JOHN 3:15 NIV

Whoever transgresses and does not abide in the doctrine of Christ does not have God. He who abides in the doctrine of Christ has both the Father and the Son.
2 JOHN 1:9 NKJV

And now, little children, abide in him; that, when he shall appear, we may have confidence, and not be ashamed before him at his coming.
1 JOHN 2:28 KJV

# 2

## Addiction

An addiction is an activity repeated so frequently that it becomes very difficult to break free from it. Either that or a person has an inborn weakness for something—say, alcohol—and is hooked after even the first drink.

The Bible talks a great deal about the dangers of alcoholism, and had illegal drugs, tobacco, and pornography existed back then, it would have mentioned them as well.

Some men are also addicted to gambling or to extramarital sex because of the stimulation and the rush these things give them.

Many find the effort to resist sinful urges so difficult that they hide behind excuses such as "I can't help it. I'm genetically hardwired to give in to these things." No. We may have an inborn weakness in a certain area, or a tendency toward certain sinful activities, but we always have a choice.

It takes prayer and faithfully, repeatedly resisting temptation and fighting such urges, but God's Spirit can help us overcome.

Do not join those who drink too much wine or gorge themselves on meat, for drunkards and gluttons become poor, and drowsiness clothes them in rags.
PROVERBS 23:20–21 NIV

Don't be drunk with wine, because that will ruin your life. Instead, be filled with the Holy Spirit.
EPHESIANS 5:18 NLT

Let us behave decently, as in the daytime, not in carousing and drunkenness, not in sexual immorality and debauchery, not in dissension and jealousy.
ROMANS 13:13 NIV

*Of all vices, drinking is the most incompatible with greatness.*
WALTER SCOTT

Jesus answered them, "Truly, truly, I say to you, everyone who commits sin is the slave of sin."
JOHN 8:34 NASB

*When any small adversity befalleth us, we are too quickly dejected, and turn ourselves to human comforts. If we would endeavor, like men of courage, to stand in the battle, surely we should feel the favorable assistance of God from heaven.*
THOMAS À KEMPIS

Therefore, dear brothers and sisters, you have no obligation to do what your sinful nature urges you to do. For if you live by its dictates, you will die. But if through the power of the Spirit you put to death the deeds of your sinful nature, you will live. For all who are led by the Spirit of God are children of God.
ROMANS 8:12–14 NLT

When you follow the desires of your sinful nature, the results are very clear: sexual immorality, impurity, lustful pleasures, idolatry, sorcery, hostility, quarreling, jealousy, outbursts of anger, selfish ambition, dissension, division, envy, drunkenness, wild parties, and other sins like these. Let me tell you again, as I have before, that anyone living that sort of life will not inherit the Kingdom of God.
GALATIANS 5:19–21 NLT

Do not let sin control the way you live;
do not give in to sinful desires.
ROMANS 6:12 NLT

But if you do not do what is right, sin is crouching at your door; it desires to have you, but you must rule over it.
GENESIS 4:7 NIV

> *Sin is a sovereign till sovereign grace dethrones it.*
> CHARLES H. SPURGEON

If the Son gives you freedom, you are free!
JOHN 8:36 CEV

There hath no temptation taken you but such as is common to man: but God is faithful, who will not suffer you to be tempted above that ye are able; but will with the temptation also make a way to escape, that ye may be able to bear it.
1 CORINTHIANS 10:13 KJV

When people sin, you should forgive and comfort them, so they won't give up in despair.
2 CORINTHIANS 2:7 CEV

# 3

## Ambition

Ambition can be a very good thing. According to the dictionary it is "the determination to achieve success or distinction." To be ambitious is to be "strongly determined." When you have a vision and a goal, it inspires you to work hard and achieve excellence.

You need a healthy dose of ambition if you're studying a career in college or starting a new business. If you have no ambition you'll just drift through life.

But there is a dark side to ambition. We've all heard of men so narrowly focused on succeeding that they sacrifice everything on the altar of ambition—their marriage, their family, their health, and their soul.

That is why you must pursue God's goals, and even then, not become so obsessed with "succeeding" that you get life out of balance.

The key is to submit all your plans to God for His approval, then constantly come to Him for direction and wisdom so you can make that ambition come true.

Also, make it your ambition to live quietly, to mind your own business and to earn your living by your own efforts— just as we told you.
1 THESSALONIANS 4:11 CJB

I realized that it's good and proper for a man to eat and drink. It's good for him to be satisfied with his hard work on this earth. That's what he should do during the few days of life God has given him.
ECCLESIASTES 5:18 NIrV

*Ambition has been called one of the major ingredients*
*for keeping people from aging.*
WILLIAM KRUTZA

Lazy people want much but get little, but those who
work hard will prosper.
PROVERBS 13:4 NLT

Lazy people finally die of hunger because they won't
get up and go to work.
PROVERBS 21:25 MSG

He who tills his land will have plenty of bread, but he who
follows frivolity will have poverty enough!
PROVERBS 28:19 NKJV

We work to feed our appetites; meanwhile our souls go hungry.
ECCLESIASTES 6:7 MSG

*Ambition must be tempered by self-control. It isn't somebody else's job*
*to hold your ambition in check.*
MARK ELFSTRAND

But as for you, do you seek great things for yourself?
Stop seeking!
JEREMIAH 45:5 HCSB

People who want to be rich fall into all sorts of temptations and
traps. They are caught by foolish and harmful desires that drag
them down and destroy them. The love of money causes all
kinds of trouble.
1 TIMOTHY 6:9–10 CEV

*What's my goal? What's my ambition?*
*Is it my happiness or my holiness?*
KAY ARTHUR

Now listen, you who say, "Today or tomorrow we will go to this or that city, spend a year there, carry on business and make money." Why, you do not even know what will happen tomorrow. . . . Instead, you ought to say, "If it is the Lord's will, we will live and do this or that."
JAMES 4:13–15 NIV

Do nothing out of selfish ambition or vain conceit.
Rather, in humility value others above yourselves.
PHILIPPIANS 2:3 NIV

For where you have envy and selfish ambition, there you find disorder and every evil practice.
JAMES 3:16 NIV

*To have peace with God one must intentionally die to self,*
*to all self-ambition, until you are only living for Jesus.*
KATHRYN KUHLMAN

# 4

## Anger

The Bible has a great deal to say about anger. That's because it is very human to become impatient and frustrated with others and to express those feelings with heated words.

Likewise, when we feel that we have been slighted or treated unjustly, it's a natural reaction to become heated under the collar.

There are certainly times when we're justified in being angry—in fact, flagrant injustice ought to upset us. This kind of anger is referred to as "righteous indignation."

Most of the time, however, there is nothing righteous at all about us letting off steam. The Bible says, "the wrath of man does not produce the righteousness of God" (James 1:20 NKJV).

We must learn to control our temper—otherwise anger will rage out of control and cause us to say and do hurtful things. Words blurted out in anger are often long regretted.

True, we may have been born with a quick temper, but God can still help us master it.

Let go of anger, and leave rage behind. Do not be preoccupied. It only leads to evil.
PSALM 37:8 GW

Whoever is patient has great understanding, but one who is quick-tempered displays folly.
PROVERBS 14:29 NIV

*The peculiarity of ill temper is that it is the vice of the virtuous. It is often the one blot on an otherwise noble character.*
HENRY DRUMMOND

People with quick tempers cause trouble, but those who control their tempers stop a quarrel.
PROVERBS 15:18 NCV

Whoever is slow to anger is better than the mighty, and he who rules his spirit than he who takes a city.
PROVERBS 16:32 ESV

Good sense makes one slow to anger, and it is his glory to overlook an offense.
PROVERBS 19:11 ESV

> *Allowing anger to seethe on the back burner will lead to a very large lid blowing off a very hot pot.*
> CHARLES SWINDOLL

But now you must stop doing such things. You must quit being angry, hateful, and evil. You must no longer say insulting or cruel things about others.
COLOSSIANS 3:8 CEV

Like grabbing a dog by the ears, so is a bystander who gets involved in someone else's quarrel.
PROVERBS 26:17 GW

An angry man stirs up strife, and a furious man abounds in transgression.
PROVERBS 29:22 NKJV

Let all bitterness, and wrath, and anger, and clamour, and evil speaking, be put away from you, with all malice.
EPHESIANS 4:31 KJV

*When anger wins, love always loses.*
WILLARD HARLEY JR.

Everyone should be quick to listen, slow to speak and slow
to become angry, because our anger does not produce the
righteousness that God desires.
JAMES 1:19–20 TNIV

And "don't sin by letting anger control you." Don't let the sun go
down while you are still angry.
EPHESIANS 4:26 NLT

*We all get angry, and at times we should. What's important
is that we find constructive outlets for that anger.*
MORT CRIM

Now when Rachel saw that she bore Jacob no children, she. . .
said to Jacob, "Give me children, or else I die." Then Jacob's
anger burned against Rachel, and he said, "Am I in the place of
God, who has withheld from you the fruit of the womb?"
GENESIS 30:1–2 NASB

# 5

*Backsliding*

You don't hear the term *backslider* used too much in churches today—although the condition it describes is still around.

Today we're more apt to say that someone is no longer walking with the Lord or that they have fallen by the wayside. Or we may take part of the blame for their fall, confessing that we "let them slip through the cracks."

For whatever reason—and there are many—Christians sometimes lose their initial, ardent love for God. They no longer believe, or strive to live, their faith.

They may openly slide back into their former lifestyle, even openly speak against their former faith. Or they may continue attending church, outwardly living a moral life, but be spiritually cold and/or secretly indulging in sin.

We should be charitable toward backsliders knowing that we, too, have backslidden at times—or even just in a specific area.

We should also remember that God loves the fallen, longs for fellowship with them, and implores them to return.

For, as I have often told you before and now tell you again even with tears, many live as enemies of the cross of Christ. Their destiny is destruction, their god is their stomach, and their glory is in their shame. Their mind is set on earthly things.
PHILIPPIANS 3:18–19 NIV

"Your own wickedness will correct you, and your backslidings will rebuke you. Know therefore and see that it is an evil and bitter thing that you have forsaken the LORD your God, and the fear of Me is not in you," says the Lord GOD of hosts.
JEREMIAH 2:19 NKJV

For if after they have escaped the pollutions of the world through the knowledge of the Lord and Saviour Jesus Christ, they are again entangled therein, and overcome, the latter end is worse with them than the beginning. For it had been better for them not to have known the way of righteousness, than, after they have known it, to turn from the holy commandment delivered unto them. But it is happened unto them according to the true proverb, The dog is turned to his own vomit again; and the sow that was washed to her wallowing in the mire.

2 PETER 2:20–22 KJV

*For every one that definitely turns his back on Christ, there are hundreds who drift from him. Life's ocean is full of currents, any one of which will sweep us past the harbor-mouth even when we seem nearest to it, and carry us far out to sea.*

F. B. MEYER

*Man-like is it to fall into sin,*
*Fiend-like is it to dwell therein;*
*Christ-like is it for sin to grieve,*
*God-like is it all sin to leave.*

FRIEDRICH, FREIHERR VON LOGAU

Go and proclaim these words toward the north, and say: "Return, backsliding Israel," says the LORD; "I will not cause My anger to fall on you. For I am merciful," says the LORD; "I will not remain angry forever. Only acknowledge your iniquity, that you have transgressed against the LORD your God and you have not obeyed My voice," says the LORD. "Return, O backsliding children," says the LORD; "for I am married to you."

JEREMIAH 3:12–14 NKJV

Backsliders get what they deserve;
good people receive their reward.
PROVERBS 14:14 NLT

If my people, who are called by my name, will humble themselves
and pray and seek my face and turn from their wicked ways,
then I will hear from heaven, and I will forgive their sin and will
heal their land.
2 CHRONICLES 7:14 NIV

*Before we can begin to see the cross as something done for us,*
*we have to see it as something done by us.*
JOHN STOTT

I know what you have done—how hard you have worked and
how you have endured. . . . However, I have this against you: The
love you had at first is gone. Remember how far you have fallen.
Return to me and change the way you think and act, and do what
you did at first. I will come to you and take your lamp stand from
its place if you don't change.
REVELATION 2:2, 4–5 GW

They will never again pollute themselves with their idols and
vile images and rebellion, for I will save them from their sinful
backsliding. I will cleanse them. Then they will truly be my
people, and I will be their God.
EZEKIEL 37:23 NLT

*Sin and dandelions are a whole lot alike—*
*they're a lifetime fight that you never quite win.*
WILLIAM ALLEN WHITE

# 6

## Blessings

God repeatedly promises to bless His children, and this is, frankly, one of our chief motivations for following and obeying Him. We want to be blessed.

Often these blessings are material. After all, God knows that we need food to eat, clothes to wear, and a place to live. In the Old Testament, God's people considered themselves particularly blessed if they had these things in abundance.

Like us today, they also considered themselves blessed if they had good health, obedient children, and were spared during disasters and times of danger.

In the New Testament, Jesus came to save us from hell, the ultimate danger, and to bring us the ultimate blessing—eternal life in heaven.

He also taught us that just because we're poor, hungry, and persecuted, that doesn't mean that we aren't blessed. We're just as surely blessed—we just have to wait 'til we get to heaven to receive our reward.

In the meantime, we're blessed with peace and joy.

The LORD had said to Abram, "Leave your native country, your relatives, and your father's family, and go to the land that I will show you. I will make you into a great nation. I will bless you and make you famous, and you will be a blessing to others. I will bless those who bless you and curse those who treat you with contempt. All the families on earth will be blessed through you."
GENESIS 12:1–3 NLT

LORD, you alone are my inheritance, my cup of blessing.
You guard all that is mine.
PSALM 16:5 NLT

*If our only blessings were possessions, in heaven we would be the
poorest of souls. But because God made Himself our best blessing,
we are rich both here and for eternity.*

Then Jesus turned to his disciples and said, "God blesses you
who are poor, for the Kingdom of God is yours. God blesses
you who are hungry now, for you will be satisfied. God blesses
you who weep now, for in due time you will laugh. What blessings await you when people hate you and exclude you and mock
you and curse you as evil because you follow the Son of Man.
When that happens, be happy! Yes, leap for joy! For a great
reward awaits you in heaven."
LUKE 6:20–23 NLT

But I say to you who hear, love your enemies, do good to those
who hate you, bless those who curse you, pray for those who
mistreat you.
LUKE 6:27–28 NASB

*To love God is the greatest of virtues;
to be loved by God is the greatest of blessings.*
UNKNOWN

The LORD bless you, and keep you; the LORD make His face shine
on you, and be gracious to you; the LORD lift up His countenance
on you, and give you peace.
NUMBERS 6:24–26 NASB

LORD, you are mine! I promise to obey your words! With all
my heart I want your blessings. Be merciful as you promised.
I pondered the direction of my life, and I turned to follow
your laws.
PSALM 119:57–59 NLT

From his abundance we have all received one
gracious blessing after another.
JOHN 1:16 NLT

*Not only does God bless us, we bless others*
*as we share His blessings with them.*

Do not repay evil with evil or insult with insult. On the contrary,
repay evil with blessing, because to this you were called so that
you may inherit a blessing.
1 PETER 3:9 NIV

# 7

## Brothers

The Bible calls fellow believers "brothers" and tells Christians to "love as brothers" (1 Peter 3:8 NKJV). Brothers, ideally, are loyal. They stand with each other through both easy times and adversity.

They were literally born for that purpose.

We are in a spiritual war, and God knew that men who strive to live the Christian life would, at times, face severe testing and battles. That's why we need a band of brothers—whether actual brothers or friends as loyal as a brother.

The Church at large is meant to fulfill this role. Still, every man needs a small group of godly men whom he can count on to support him, pray for him, and counsel him.

We all need like-minded buddies to hang out and relax with. But being a brother goes deeper than that. Brothers don't give up on each other. They answer that phone call at midnight.

Be a brother to other Christian men, and seek out brothers to walk with you.

A friend always loves, and a brother is born to share trouble.
PROVERBS 17:17 GW

How good and pleasant it is when God's people
live together in unity!
PSALM 133:1 NIV

Two are better than one because they have a good return for their labor. For if either of them falls, the one will lift up his companion. But woe to the one who falls when there is not another to lift him up.
ECCLESIASTES 4:9–10 NASB

*You can't do life alone, and you don't have to. Life is meant to be a partnership, lived in community with family and friends.*
STAN TOLER

One person could be overpowered. But two people can stand up for themselves. And a rope made out of three cords isn't easily broken.
ECCLESIASTES 4:12 NIrV

And five of you shall chase an hundred, and an hundred of you shall put ten thousand to flight: and your enemies shall fall before you by the sword.
LEVITICUS 26:8 KJV

Jonathan said to his young armor-bearer, "Come, let's go over to the outpost of those uncircumcised fellows. Perhaps the LORD will act in our behalf. Nothing can hinder the LORD from saving, whether by many or by few." "Do all that you have in mind," his armor-bearer said. "Go ahead; I am with you heart and soul."
1 SAMUEL 14:6–7 TNIV

*No man is an island, entire of itself;*
*every man is a piece of the continent, a part of the main.*
JOHN DONNE

Now when he departed from there, he met Jehonadab the son of Rechab, coming to meet him; and he greeted him and said to him, "Is your heart right, as my heart is toward your heart?" And Jehonadab answered, "It is." Jehu said, "If it is, give me your hand." So he gave him his hand, and he took him up to him into the chariot.
2 KINGS 10:15 NKJV

Can two walk together, except they be agreed?
AMOS 3:3 KJV

Finally, brothers and sisters, rejoice! Strive for full restoration,
encourage one another, be of one mind, live in peace.
2 CORINTHIANS 13:11 NIV

*Say not "Our Father," and then look upon thy brethren with a sneer or*
*a frown. I beseech thee, live like a brother, and act like a brother.*
CHARLES H. SPURGEON

Now when he had finished speaking to Saul, the soul of Jonathan
was knit to the soul of David, and Jonathan loved him
as his own soul.
1 SAMUEL 18:1 NKJV

David asked Ahimelech the Hittite and Joab's brother Abishai,
"Which one of you will go with me into Saul's camp?"
"I will!" Abishai answered.
1 SAMUEL 26:6 CEV

How beloved and gracious were Saul and Jonathan! They were
together in life and in death. They were swifter than eagles,
stronger than lions.
2 SAMUEL 1:23 NLT

Be devoted to one another in love.
Honor one another above yourselves.
ROMANS 12:10 NIV

# 8

## Church

The Greek word for "church," *ekklesia*, means "that which is called out"—literally, God's people who have been called out of the world to follow Jesus.

For the first three centuries of Christian history, the Church met wherever they could—usually in people's homes. Nevertheless, it makes sense these days to have designated buildings where large numbers of Christians can gather.

We, the Church, are the Body of Christ on the earth. Christ Himself is our head. All genuine believers, regardless of denomination, belong to the one, true Church.

Church happens wherever two or more believers gather— and it is God's will that we gather together regularly, at least once a week, to hear God's Word, to worship Him, and to encourage one another.

Our salvation is determined by our personal relationship with the Lord, and simply attending a church won't save us. However, it's definitely God's will for the individual members to come together and be united.

We all belong to one Body, after all.

For where two or three are gathered together in my name, there am I in the midst of them.
MATTHEW 18:20 KJV

God has put all things under the authority of Christ and has made him head over all things for the benefit of the church. And the church is his body; it is made full and complete by Christ, who fills all things everywhere with himself.
EPHESIANS 1:22–23 NLT

Christ also loved the church and gave Himself for her, that He might sanctify and cleanse her with the washing of water by the word, that He might present her to Himself a glorious church, not having spot or wrinkle or any such thing, but that she should be holy and without blemish.

EPHESIANS 5:25–27 NKJV

*The Christian does not go to the temple to worship. The Christian takes the temple with him or her. Jesus lifts us beyond the building and pays the human body the highest compliment by making it His dwelling place, the place where He meets with us.*

RAVI ZACHARIAS

Now these are the gifts Christ gave to the church: the apostles, the prophets, the evangelists, and the pastors and teachers. Their responsibility is to equip God's people to do his work and build up the church, the body of Christ.

EPHESIANS 4:11–12 NLT

What if he refuses to listen even to the church? Then don't treat him as your brother. Treat him as you would treat an ungodly person or a tax collector.

MATTHEW 18:17 NIrV

We will speak the truth in love, growing in every way more and more like Christ, who is the head of his body, the church. He makes the whole body fit together perfectly. As each part does its own special work, it helps the other parts grow, so that the whole body is healthy and growing and full of love.

EPHESIANS 4:15–16 NLT

*The uniqueness of the church is her message—the Gospel. The church is the only institution entrusted by God with the message of repentance of sins and belief in Jesus Christ for forgiveness.*
MARK DEVER AND PAUL ALEXANDER

My friends, I beg you to watch out for anyone who causes trouble and divides the church by refusing to do what all of you were taught. Stay away from them!
ROMANS 16:17 CEV

*A church should be a power-house, where sluggish spirits can get recharged and reanimated.*
SAMUEL A. ELIOT

But God composed the body, having given greater honor to that part which lacks it, that there should be no schism in the body, but that the members should have the same care for one another. And if one member suffers, all the members suffer with it; or if one member is honored, all the members rejoice with it. Now you are the body of Christ, and members individually.
1 CORINTHIANS 12:24–27 NKJV

# 9

*Citizenship*

As citizens of the country we live in, we know that we have certain inalienable rights. This is particularly true if we live in a democracy or a nation under a stable rule of law.

The apostle Paul was a Roman citizen, and he knew and quoted his rights to the authorities on at least two occasions— and probably more.

But with rights come responsibilities: the same law that confers privileges on us also sets limitations on our behavior, in the interest of protecting others' rights.

The law also makes certain demands, requiring us to pay taxes, obey traffic rules, and conduct business within legal and ethical guidelines.

As Christians, we hold dual citizenship: we are first and foremost citizens of the Kingdom of God. While our heavenly citizenship supersedes all other loyalties, it should make us even better citizens of our earthly nation.

God wants us to be a good example of His love in a fallen world, so we should be careful to obey the laws of the land.

Let every soul be subject to the governing authorities. For there is no authority except from God, and the authorities that exist are appointed by God. Therefore whoever resists the authority resists the ordinance of God, and those who resist will bring judgment on themselves.
ROMANS 13:1–2 NKJV

Remind the people to be subject to rulers and authorities, to be obedient, to be ready to do whatever is good.
TITUS 3:1 TNIV

*Whatever makes men good Christians makes them good citizens.*
DANIEL WEBSTER

You must also pay your taxes. The authorities are God's servants, and it is their duty to take care of these matters. Pay all that you owe, whether it is taxes and fees or respect and honor.
ROMANS 13:6–7 CEV

And He said to them, "Render therefore to Caesar the things that are Caesar's, and to God the things that are God's."
MATTHEW 22:21 NKJV

Therefore submit yourselves to every ordinance of man for the Lord's sake, whether to the king as supreme, or to governors, as to those who are sent by him.
1 PETER 2:13–14 NKJV

And work for the peace and prosperity of the city where I sent you into exile. Pray to the LORD for it, for its welfare will determine your welfare.
JEREMIAH 29:7 NLT

*Pray for the city you live in right now and its people, for its welfare and your welfare. This is one of the fundamental keys. As you become a blessing, you set yourself up to be blessed.*
TONY EVANS

I exhort therefore, that. . .prayers, intercessions, and giving of thanks, be made for all men; for kings, and for all that are in authority; that we may lead a quiet and peaceable life in all godliness and honesty.
1 TIMOTHY 2:1–2 KJV

A commander was standing there as they stretched Paul out to
be whipped. Paul said to him, "Does the law allow you to whip
a Roman citizen who hasn't even been found guilty?". . .
Right away those who were about to question him left.
Even the officer was alarmed. He realized that he had put Paul,
a Roman citizen, in chains.
ACTS 22:25, 29 NIRV

> *The fact that we have our citizenship in heaven ought to make us*
> *better citizens on earth, no matter under what form*
> *of government we may live.*
> WARREN W. WIERSBE

Remember that at that time you were separate from Christ,
excluded from citizenship in Israel and foreigners to the
covenants of the promise. . .But now in Christ Jesus you who
once were far away have been brought near by the
blood of Christ.
EPHESIANS 2:12–13 NIV

Now therefore ye are no more strangers and foreigners, but
fellow citizens with the saints, and of the household of God.
EPHESIANS 2:19 KJV

> *Christians must not forget their identity: Christians are first and*
> *foremost citizens of the Kingdom of Heaven.*
> FRANKLIN GRAHAM

But our citizenship is in heaven. And we eagerly await a Savior
from there, the Lord Jesus Christ.
PHILIPPIANS 3:20 NIV

# 10

*Comfort*

When the Bible speaks of God comforting us, it means that He consoles us or gives us relief in our troubles. He is aware of what we are going through and He cares.

This doesn't mean that He necessarily disposes of our problems, dispels all the pressures that beset us, and makes us completely comfortable. It means that He's with us in our afflictions and puts His arms around us.

God's comfort is reserved for those who are suffering or sorrowful. Those who are comfortable and complacent have no need of it.

The word most frequently used in the New Testament for "comfort" means "to come alongside." This is what the Holy Spirit does, so although other translations call Him the Helper or the Counselor, the King James Version refers to Him as the Comforter.

Life is not easy, and at certain times we feel distressed and miserable indeed. That's when God comes to us and—if we let Him—gives us hope and comfort.

Shout for joy, you heavens; rejoice, you earth; burst into song, you mountains! For the LORD comforts his people and will have compassion on his afflicted ones.
ISAIAH 49:13 NIV

*Comfort is not the absence of problems;*
*comfort is the strength to face my problems.*
KEN HUTCHERSON

Even though I walk through the darkest valley, I will fear no evil, for you are with me; your rod and your staff, they comfort me.
PSALM 23:4 NIV

You have allowed me to suffer much hardship, but you will restore me to life again and lift me up from the depths of the earth. You will restore me to even greater honor and comfort me once again.
PSALM 71:20–21 NLT

Give me a sign of your goodness, that my enemies may see it and be put to shame, for you, LORD, have helped me and comforted me.
PSALM 86:17 NIV

*If you look for truth, you may find comfort in the end; if you look for comfort you will not get either comfort or truth.*
C. S. LEWIS

Remember the word to Your servant, in which You have made me hope. This is my comfort in my affliction, that Your word has revived me.
PSALM 119:49–50 NASB

God blesses those people who grieve. They will find comfort!
MATTHEW 5:4 CEV

But the Comforter, which is the Holy Ghost, whom the Father will send in my name, he shall teach you all things, and bring all things to your remembrance, whatsoever I have said unto you.
JOHN 14:26 KJV

*There is a difference between receiving comfort and being comfortable. God's comfort comes to those who suffer for their faith, not those who are resting on their laurels.*

Christ encourages you, and his love comforts you.
PHILIPPIANS 2:1 CEV

I serve you, LORD. Comfort me with your love,
just as you have promised.
PSALM 119:76 CEV


Praise be to the God and Father of our Lord Jesus Christ, the
Father of compassion and the God of all comfort, who comforts
us in all our troubles, so that we can comfort those in any trouble
with the comfort we ourselves receive from God. For just as we
share abundantly in the sufferings of Christ, so also our comfort
abounds through Christ.
2 CORINTHIANS 1:3–5 NIV


*The world hardly knows the meaning of comfort. But the Spirit of*
*God offers the best there is to have. When we come to Him in pain and*
*faith, He touches our hearts in tender ways that no human can.*

God our Father loves us. He is kind and has given us eternal
comfort and a wonderful hope.
2 THESSALONIANS 2:16 CEV

# II

*Compassion*

The Bible describes the tender compassion that we as fathers have toward our children—or ought to have. We know that they're only children after all, and we take that into account when they've disobeyed and we're deciding how to discipline them.

God is the same way toward us: despite our often failings, despite the fact that surely we ought to know better, He restrains Himself because He remembers that we are weak.

He chastises us, but He tempers His discipline with compassion.

Yet, despite the fact that God often punishes us less than we deserve, when we see our fellow man make a mistake or sin, we want to lower the boom. When he stumbles, we stand back and let him "stew in his own juice."

Sometimes we fail to show compassion because we don't want to appear soft or weak. Yet God constantly shows compassion—and it only enhances our appreciation of Him.

We need to become more like God. We need more compassion.

[Mankind's] heart was not steadfast toward Him, nor were they faithful in His covenant. But He, being compassionate, forgave their iniquity and did not destroy them; and often He restrained His anger and did not arouse all His wrath. Thus He remembered that they were but flesh, a wind that passes and does not return.
PSALM 78:37–39 NASB

A father is tender and kind to his children. In the same way, the Lord is tender and kind to those who have respect for him.
PSALM 103:13 NIrV

*Man may dismiss compassion from his heart, but God never will.*
WILLIAM COWPER

The Lord is compassionate and gracious, slow to anger and abounding in lovingkindness. He will not always strive with us, nor will He keep His anger forever.
Psalm 103:8–9 NASB

Shout for joy, you heavens; rejoice, you earth; burst into song, you mountains! For the Lord comforts his people and will have compassion on his afflicted ones.
Isaiah 49:13 NIV

Have mercy upon me, O God, according to thy lovingkindness: according unto the multitude of thy tender mercies blot out my transgressions.
Psalm 51:1 KJV

> *Christianity demands a level of caring that*
> *transcends human inclinations.*
> Erwin W. Lutzer

Whoever covers over his sins does not prosper. Whoever confesses and abandons them receives compassion.
Proverbs 28:13 GW

So the Lord must wait for you to come to him so he can show you his love and compassion. For the Lord is a faithful God. Blessed are those who wait for his help.
Isaiah 30:18 NLT

For no one is abandoned by the Lord forever. Though he brings grief, he also shows compassion because of the greatness of his unfailing love. For he does not enjoy hurting people or causing them sorrow.
Lamentations 3:31–33 NLT

*Biblical orthodoxy without compassion is surely
the ugliest thing in the world.*
FRANCIS SCHAEFFER

You must be compassionate, just as your Father
is compassionate.
LUKE 6:36 NLT

If anyone has this world's goods and sees his brother in need but
shuts off his compassion from him—how can God's love
reside in him?
1 JOHN 3:17 HCSB

Light shines in the darkness for the godly. They are generous,
compassionate, and righteous.
PSALM 112:4 NLT

# 12

## Competitiveness

There are always exceptions, but men in general like to win.

Life often becomes a contest to make the most money, earn the greatest respect, and marry the most attractive woman. The guys higher up the ladder look down on the poor guys below, who look back up with mixed admiration and envy.

Is that the way God intended it?

No. Although Paul often compared the Christian life to a race—which is surely a competitive event—this race is against ourselves, not against the people around us. We strive against our own sinful desires and bad habits that drag us down.

We are trying to give our utmost, run in our own best time, and stay on track no matter what others are doing. We are not to compare ourselves to anyone else.

In fact, the true winners are those who take the time to reach out to others, pick them up when they stumble, and encourage them to excel in their race.

Each one should test their own actions. Then they can take pride in themselves alone, without comparing themselves to someone else.
GALATIANS 6:4 NIV

If we live in the Spirit, let us also walk in the Spirit. Let us not be desirous of vain glory, provoking one another,
envying one another.
GALATIANS 5:25–26 KJV

For we dare not class ourselves or compare ourselves with those who commend themselves. But they, measuring themselves by themselves, and comparing themselves among themselves,
are not wise.
2 CORINTHIANS 10:12 NKJV

*Father, it's so easy to compare—to think too highly of myself,*
*or too low. Help me see myself as You do.*

It is obvious what kind of life develops out of trying to get your
own way all the time. . .cutthroat competition; all-consuming-
yet-never-satisfied wants. . .the vicious habit of depersonalizing
everyone into a rival; uncontrolled and uncontrollable addictions;
ugly parodies of community.
GALATIANS 5:19–21 MSG

Do nothing out of selfish ambition or vain conceit. Rather, in
humility value others above yourselves, not looking to your own
interests but each of you to the interests of others.
PHILIPPIANS 2:3–4 NIV

*The Christian life is not a competition with others;*
*we have a common goal and we grow together in the strength*
*and grace of the body of believers.*
GEORGE VERWER

Loners who care only for themselves spit on the common good.
PROVERBS 18:1 MSG

Carry each other's burdens, and in this way you will fulfill the
law of Christ.
GALATIANS 6:2 NIV

But may it never be that I would boast, except in the cross of our
Lord Jesus Christ, through which the world has been crucified to
me, and I to the world.
GALATIANS 6:14 NASB

*Lord, keep my eyes off "the other guy"—*
*and always on You and Your Son, Jesus.*

Therefore, since we are surrounded by so great a cloud of witnesses, let us also lay aside every weight, and sin which clings so closely, and let us run with endurance the race that is set before us, looking to Jesus, the founder and perfecter of our faith, who for the joy that was set before him endured the cross, despising the shame, and is seated at the right hand of the throne of God.
HEBREWS 12:1–2 ESV

We should all please our neighbors for their good, to build them up.
ROMANS 15:2 TNIV

# 13

## Complaining

The first books of the Bible contain account after account of the Israelites murmuring about the troubles they faced in the desert and griping against Moses' leadership. They even complained about God's provision.

No sooner was one situation resolved than they complained about another.

And yet we see, time and again, God coming through for them—so they could've saved themselves all the grumbling. Either that or God judged them for the serious sin of murmuring, because it revealed their doubt and bitterness toward Him.

So we wonder, "Why on earth didn't they learn?"

And yet we bellyache to coworkers about our boss and job conditions, complain about the service we receive—even murmur to God about our finances—and think that we have every right to feel the way we do.

When will we ever learn?

God knows that we're all tempted to doubt and fret and complain. That's why He gives us the antidote: to trust Him, to be content, and to praise Him.

*God of all comfort, keep me from complaining if my burden seems heavy. Help me to follow in Your footsteps and endure every weakness without the sin of resentment or complaint.*
JONI EARECKSON TADA

In the desert the whole community grumbled against Moses and Aaron. The Israelites said to them, "If only we had died. . .in Egypt! There we sat around pots of meat and ate all the food we wanted, but you have brought us out into this desert to starve this entire assembly to death."
EXODUS 16:2–3 TNIV

This evening you will know that it is GOD who brought you out of Egypt. . .Yes, he's listened to your complaints against him. You haven't been complaining against us, you know, but against GOD.
EXODUS 16:6–7 MSG

And the people thirsted there for water, and the people complained against Moses, and said, "Why is it you have brought us up out of Egypt, to kill us and our children and livestock with thirst?"
EXODUS 17:3 NKJV

*Those who choose complaining as their lifestyle will spend their lifetime in the wilderness. Complaining is sin.*
JAMES MACDONALD

Do everything without grumbling or arguing.
PHILIPPIANS 2:14 NIV

Let the peace that Christ gives control your thinking, because you were all called together in one body to have peace.
Always be thankful.
COLOSSIANS 3:15 NCV

"If only we had died in Egypt, or even here in the wilderness!" they complained. "Why is the LORD taking us to this country only to have us die in battle? Our wives and our little ones will be carried off as plunder!"
NUMBERS 14:2–3 NLT

Then they refused to go into the beautiful land of Canaan; they did not believe what God promised. They grumbled in their tents and did not obey the LORD.
PSALM 106:24–25 NCV

Yet, God was not pleased with most of them, so their dead
bodies were scattered over the desert. Don't complain as some
of them did.
1 CORINTHIANS 10:5, 10 GW

*If you think you accomplish anything positive by complaining or
nagging, God's Word says otherwise. By complaining, you just put
yourself in judgment's way.*
RHONDA RIZZO WEBB

In every thing give thanks: for this is the will of God
in Christ Jesus concerning you.
1 THESSALONIANS 5:18 KJV

*For as thankfulness is an express acknowledgement of the goodness of
God towards you, so repining and complaints are as plain accusations
of want of God's goodness towards you.*
WILLIAM LAW

I cry aloud to the LORD; I lift up my voice to the LORD for mercy.
I pour out before him my complaint; before him I tell my trouble.
PSALM 142:1–2 NIV

# 14

## Conversation

Apart from how you live, what you say and the way you say it is the clearest way of communicating to others who you are. This holds true whether you're a real conversationalist or a man of few words, the town clown or sober and serious.

You may be able to hold in your real attitudes for a long while, but eventually you'll put words to the things that you spend the most time thinking about.

That's why the Bible tells us to think about good, pure things, and to fill our hearts with wholesome thoughts.

As men, we're sometimes tempted to tell an off-color joke or use coarse language to fit in with the guys and show them that we're "just like them." But they need to know that being a Christian makes a difference.

It may take awhile to let God gain control of your tongue and master your words, but easy or not, this is what God desires.

Put away from you a deceitful mouth, and put perverse lips far from you.
PROVERBS 4:24 NKJV

My advice is wholesome. There is nothing devious or crooked in it.
PROVERBS 8:8 NLT

Wise people store up knowledge. But the mouths of foolish people destroy them.
PROVERBS 10:14 NIrV

*Our words reveal our character.*
RHONDA RIZZO

Let your speech be always with grace.
COLOSSIANS 4:6 KJV

Go from the presence of a foolish man, when you do not
perceive in him the lips of knowledge.
PROVERBS 14:7 NKJV

Don't pay any attention to that godless and stupid talk that
sounds smart but really isn't.
1 TIMOTHY 6:20 CEV

A wholesome tongue is a tree of life; but perverseness therein
is a breach in the spirit.
PROVERBS 15:4 KJV

*God intends for the words of His church to touch the world. And when*
*we speak lovingly and respectfully to one another, we literally*
*identify ourselves as His disciples.*
RON MEHL

The heart of him that hath understanding seeketh knowledge:
but the mouth of fools feedeth on foolishness.
PROVERBS 15:14 KJV

The beginning of the words of his mouth is foolishness,
and the end of his talk is evil madness.
ECCLESIASTES 10:13 ESV

Do not let any unwholesome talk come out of your mouths,
but only what is helpful for building others up according to
their needs, that it may benefit those who listen.
EPHESIANS 4:29 NIV

*If I proclaim Jesus to be Lord of my life, then He's Lord of my bank account, my speech. . .my thoughts and all the minutia of details that I encounter each and every day.*
REBECCA LUSIGNOLO-McGLONE

There must not be any unclean speech or foolish talk or dirty jokes. All of them are out of place. Instead, you should give thanks.
EPHESIANS 5:4 NIrV

It wasn't long ago that you were doing all that stuff and not knowing any better. But you know better now, so make sure it's all gone for good: bad temper, irritability, meanness, profanity, dirty talk.
COLOSSIANS 3:7–8 MSG

Be gracious in your speech. The goal is to bring out the best in others in a conversation, not put them down, not cut them out.
COLOSSIANS 4:6 MSG

*Because words have the power to affect people deeply, it is appropriate to consider how to encourage fellow Christians through what we say.*
LARRY CRABB

Use clean language that no one can criticize. Do this, and your enemies will be too ashamed to say anything against you.
TITUS 2:8 CEV

# 15

## Decision Making

We are constantly called upon to make decisions—both in our private lives and in the workplace. Some decisions have far-reaching implications; others are seemingly minor.

If it's a choice between right and wrong, we generally call such decisions "resisting temptation." Where the Bible speaks clearly on moral issues, our choice is simply whether we will obey God or not.

Often, however, there are practical, not ethical, issues at stake, and we require wisdom. If we don't have enough facts to make an informed decision, we need to seek counsel.

The first thing we should do is turn to God in prayer. Often He will remind us of key facts or help us discern the real issues. Perhaps what seems to be a straightforward business decision is actually a choice between selfishness and unselfishness.

We should also have the humility to seek advice from wise and knowledgeable men. Sometimes, because they're not as embroiled in the situation as we are, they can see things more clearly.

I bless the LORD who gives me counsel;
in the night also my heart instructs me.
PSALM 16:7 ESV

You guide me with your counsel, and afterward you will
take me into glory.
PSALM 73:24 NIV

Blessed is the one who does not walk in step with the wicked
or stand in the way that sinners take or sit in the company
of mockers.
PSALM 1:1 NIV

I, wisdom, dwell with prudence, and I find knowledge and discretion. The fear of the LORD is hatred of evil. Pride and arrogance and the way of evil and perverted speech I hate. I have counsel and sound wisdom; I have insight; I have strength. By me kings reign, and rulers decree what is just.
PROVERBS 8:12–15 ESV

*In the darkest of nights cling to the assurance that God loves you, that He always has advice for you, a path that you can tread and a solution to your problem—and you will experience that which you believe.*
BASILEA SCHLINK

Then King Rehoboam consulted the elders who had served his father Solomon during his lifetime. "How would you advise me to answer these people?" he asked. They replied, "If today you will be a servant to these people and serve them and give them a favorable answer, they will always be your servants." But Rehoboam rejected the advice the elders gave him and consulted the young men who had grown up with him and were serving him.
1 KINGS 12:6–8 TNIV

The thoughts of the righteous are just; the counsels of the wicked are deceitful.
PROVERBS 12:5 ESV

*Christ told his disciples not to be anxious about tomorrow, but he never said not to consider tomorrow. Intelligent problem solving demands careful consideration of the future effects of present solutions.*
R. C. SPROUL

Fools think they know what is best, but a sensible person listens to advice.
PROVERBS 12:15 CEV

Listen to advice and accept instruction, that you may gain wisdom in the future. Many are the plans in the mind of a man, but it is the purpose of the LORD that will stand.
PROVERBS 19:20–21 ESV

Where there is no guidance, a people falls, but in an abundance of counselors there is safety.
PROVERBS 11:14 ESV

Without good advice everything goes wrong—it takes careful planning for things to go right.
PROVERBS 15:22 CEV

*When the honest, sincere Christian is faced with the decision regarding whether a thing is right or wrong, he should ask, Does it agree with all that the scripture has to say on the subject?*
CURTIS HUTSON

# 16

## Defrauding

We certainly don't like it when people deliberately cheat or shortchange us, overcharge us, or trick us into buying defective merchandise.

Even as Christians, we must put forth an effort to keep from blurting out choice names. We struggle to forgive those who defraud us. In addition, we usually speak up and seek financial compensation.

On top of it, we no longer trust them. We take our business elsewhere.

This is precisely why we should not shortchange others or cut corners with them: it hurts them the same way it hurts us. It makes them feel just as victimized.

It also affects our reputation and, very importantly, is a poor reflection upon the cause of Christ. After all, if there's one thing even unbelievers know about Christians, it is that they we're supposed to be honest.

It costs us something to be scrupulously honest in our dealings—but in the long run, having a reputation for cheating and defrauding can cost a lot more.

You know how hard I have worked for your father, but he has cheated me, changing my wages ten times.
GENESIS 31:6–7 NLT

I cannot tolerate dishonest scales and bags filled
with inaccurate weights.
MICAH 6:11 GW

You must use accurate scales when you weigh out merchandise,
and you must use full and honest measures.
DEUTERONOMY 25:13–14 NLT

*If I will lie for you, I will lie to you.*
*If I will cheat for you, I will cheat on you.*
JUSTIN LOOKADOO AND HAYLEY DIMARCO

Switching price tags and padding the expense account
are two things GOD hates.
PROVERBS 20:10 MSG

The shopper says, "That's junk—I'll take it off your hands,"
then goes off boasting of the bargain.
PROVERBS 20:14 MSG

"When you bring injured, lame or diseased animals and offer
them as sacrifices, should I accept them from your hands?"
says the LORD. "Cursed is the cheat who has an acceptable male
in his flock and vows to give it, but then sacrifices a blemished
animal to the Lord."
MALACHI 1:13–14 NIV

Do not take advantage of a hired worker who is poor and needy,
whether that worker is a fellow Israelite or a foreigner residing
in one of your towns.
DEUTERONOMY 24:14 NIV

*A less-than-honest person is somewhere between a pain and a catastrophe.*
HENRY CLOUD AND JOHN TOWNSEND

Woe to him who builds his house without righteousness and his
upper rooms without justice, who uses his neighbor's services
without pay and does not give him his wages.
JEREMIAH 22:13 NASB

[Teach slaves] not to steal from [their masters], but to show that they can be fully trusted, so that in every way they will make the teaching about God our Savior attractive.

TITUS 2:10 NIV

*No man who is corrupt, no man who condones corruption in others, can possibly do his duty by the community.*

THEODORE ROOSEVELT

The Lord spoke to Moses. He said, "Suppose a person sins by not being faithful to me. He does it by tricking his neighbors. He tricks them in connection with something they have placed in his care. He steals from them. Or he cheats them. Or he finds something they have lost and then tells a lie about it. Or he goes to court. He takes an oath and tells a lie when he witnesses about it. Or he commits any other sin like those sins. When he sins in any of those ways, he becomes guilty. He must return what he stole. He must give back what he took by cheating his neighbors. He must return what they placed in his care. He must return the lost property he found."

LEVITICUS 6:1–4 NIrV

Do not defraud or rob your neighbor.

LEVITICUS 19:13 NIV

# 17

*Dependability*

We all know what it's like to be let down, standing waiting for undelivered services or goods. Sometimes it's merely frustrating. Sometimes it causes a disaster.

All things being equal, people invariably choose the worker or company who is the most dependable. They're looking for men who can be counted on, men who will do what they said they would do, and do it on time.

Dependability is not only a sure way to get work but to get repeat work. For workers within a company, it's one of the most direct roads to advancement.

When a dependable man makes a promise, he does his best to keep that promise, even when circumstances change. He keeps his part of the bargain even when it hurts. This doesn't mean that he never picks up the phone and asks for an extension, or explains a cost overrun, but he doesn't have to do it often.

From cover to cover, the Bible urges men to be dependable and faithful.

Who then is the faithful and wise servant, whom the master has put in charge of the servants in his household to give them their food at the proper time? It will be good for that servant whose master finds him doing so when he returns.
MATTHEW 24:45–46 NIV

Anyone who can be trusted in little matters can also be trusted in important matters. But anyone who is dishonest in little matters will be dishonest in important matters.
LUKE 16:10 CEV

His master said to him, "Well done, good and faithful servant. You have been faithful over a little; I will set you over much. Enter into the joy of your master."
MATTHEW 25:23 ESV

And he said to him, "Well done, good servant! Because you have been faithful in a very little, you shall have authority over ten cities."
LUKE 19:17 ESV

*A good man is a gift to all who know him—he's dependable like the sunrise, because his goodness springs from inner strength, not outward circumstances.*
BON BARNES

Now, a person who is put in charge as a manager must be faithful.
1 CORINTHIANS 4:2 NLT

Try your best to please God and to be like him. Be faithful, loving, dependable, and gentle.
1 TIMOTHY 6:11 CEV

Who may worship in your sanctuary, LORD? Who may enter your presence on your holy hill? Those who lead blameless lives and do what is right, speaking the truth from sincere hearts. . . and keep their promises even when it hurts.
PSALM 15:1–2, 4 NLT

*The ability to make and keep promises is central to manhood. It may be trite to say that a man's word is his bond, but it is never trite to see it in action.*
STU WEBER

Do your work in the fear of GOD; be dependable and honest in your duties.
2 CHRONICLES 19:9 MSG

When he came and saw the grace of God, he was glad, and he exhorted them all to remain faithful to the Lord with steadfast purpose.
ACTS 11:23 ESV

When a man makes a vow to the LORD or takes an oath to obligate himself by a pledge, he must not break his word but must do everything he said.
NUMBERS 30:2 NIV

*What if God was only faithful when he felt like it, only dependable part of the time, only loving on special occasions? Thank goodness, He is always faithful to His own nature. The world desperately needs to see that same kind of faithfulness in our lives.*
LLOYD OGILVIE

Broken promises are worse than rain clouds that don't bring rain.
PROVERBS 25:14 CEV

You say, "If someone makes a promise with his fingers crossed, that's nothing; but if he swears with his hand on the Bible, that's serious." What ignorance! Does the leather on the Bible carry more weight than the skin on your hands?
MATTHEW 23:16–17 MSG

# 18

## Diligence

Diligence, according to the dictionary, is "a careful and persistent effort." A diligent man works conscientiously and does a job to the best of his ability. He pays attention to details. He doesn't have to constantly be making excuses for unfinished or sloppy work.

Whether he's an accountant tracking down missing funds or a mechanic working on an engine, he doesn't give up 'til he gets it right.

Being diligent doesn't mean being a perfectionist who takes forever to complete some task. Part of diligence, after all, is using time wisely. A diligent man knows the difference between getting something right and wasting time feather-dusting.

But when a job does need to be perfect, a diligent man is the one you ask to do it.

Diligent work pays off—not only with the satisfaction of a job well done, but usually financially as well. After all, a diligent man works hard and does quality work, and that pays off—if not immediately, over time.

Do you see a man skillful in his work? He will stand before kings; he will not stand before obscure men.
PROVERBS 22:29 ESV

Then this Daniel distinguished himself above the governors and satraps, because an excellent spirit was in him; and the king gave thought to setting him over the whole realm. . .because he was faithful; nor was there any error or fault found in him.
DANIEL 6:3–4 NKJV

*To do one's best every time he does anything is to increase his power
and prepare him for larger things.*
HENRY HOPKINS

The men in charge of the work were diligent, and the repairs
progressed under them. They rebuilt the temple of God according
to its original design and reinforced it.
2 CHRONICLES 24:13 NIV

Be it known to the king that we went to the province of Judah,
to the house of the great God. It is being built with huge stones,
and timber is laid in the walls. This work goes on diligently and
prospers in their hands.
EZRA 5:8 ESV

Suppose one of you has a hundred sheep and loses one of
them. Doesn't he leave the ninety-nine in the open country and
go after the lost sheep until he finds it?
LUKE 15:4 TNIV

Poor is he who works with a negligent hand, but the hand of the
diligent makes rich.
PROVERBS 10:4 NASB

"Or suppose a woman has ten silver coins and loses one.
Doesn't she light a lamp, sweep the house and search
carefully until she finds it?"
LUKE 15:8 NIV

*Be it yours, brethren, to glorify God in the sphere in which He has
placed you, by the diligent discharge of all your everyday duties.*
JOHN DAWSON

A sluggard's appetite is never filled, but the desires of the diligent are fully satisfied.
PROVERBS 13:4 NIV

Easy come, easy go, but steady diligence pays off.
PROVERBS 13:11 MSG

The plans of the diligent lead surely to plenty, but those of everyone who is hasty, surely to poverty.
PROVERBS 21:5 NKJV

> *Be active, be diligent; avoid all laziness, sloth, indolence.*
> JOHN WESLEY

Be thou diligent to know the state of thy flocks,
and look well to thy herds.
PROVERBS 27:23 KJV

But take diligent heed to do the commandment and the law, which Moses the servant of the LORD charged you, to love the LORD your God, and to walk in all his ways, and to keep his commandments, and to cleave unto him, and to serve him with all your heart and with all your soul.
JOSHUA 22:5 KJV

You have commanded us to keep Your precepts diligently.
PSALM 119:4 NKJV

Whoever diligently seeks good seeks [God's] favor,
but evil comes to him who searches for it.
PROVERBS 11:27 ESV

# 19

## Doubt

We all doubt certain things—and we should. When we read the headline, "Elvis Abducted by Aliens" at the checkout stand, we are wise to doubt. When a money-making scheme seems too good to be true, it pays to be cautious and skeptical.

Doubt becomes a vice when we are too skeptical. An attitude of constant mistrust makes us suspicious and cynical. Trust breaks down.

If we want to have a good relationship with someone, we must be able to trust them and give them the benefit of the doubt.

We are especially to have a strong, childlike trust when it comes to God. The more we realize how powerful God is, the greater is our faith in Him.

We begin by believing that He sent Jesus to die for our sins and miraculously raised Him from the dead to save us. Once we trust Him for eternal life, it's easier to also have the faith that He can do miracles in our life today.

Only simpletons believe everything they're told! The prudent carefully consider their steps.
PROVERBS 14:15 NLT

But if you have doubts about whether or not you should eat something, you are sinning if you go ahead and do it. For you are not following your convictions. If you do anything you believe is not right, you are sinning.
ROMANS 14:23 NLT

*Even the disciples doubted.*
MARY NELSON

Now when He rose early on the first day of the week, He appeared first to Mary Magdalene. . .She went and told those who had been with Him, as they mourned and wept. And when they heard that He was alive and had been seen by her, they did not believe.
MARK 16:9–11 NKJV

Later Jesus appeared to the Eleven as they were eating. He spoke firmly to them because they had no faith. They would not believe those who had seen him after he rose from the dead.
MARK 16:14 NIrV

My friends, watch out! Don't let evil thoughts or doubts make any of you turn from the living God.
HEBREWS 3:12 CEV

> *The chief reason we doubt, is that we don't appreciate the God we're dealing with.*
> JERRY DUNN

But Abraham never doubted or questioned God's promise. His faith made him strong, and he gave all the credit to God.
ROMANS 4:20 CEV

Truly I tell you, if anyone says to this mountain, "Go, throw yourself into the sea," and does not doubt in their heart but believes that what they say will happen, it will be done for them.
MARK 11:23 NIV

When doubts filled my mind, your comfort gave me renewed hope and cheer.
PSALM 94:19 NLT

*The whole point is not not ever doubting or questioning. It is that we walk it through and we find our God faithful.*
BETH MOORE

If any of you lacks wisdom, you should ask God, who gives generously to all without finding fault, and it will be given to you. But when you ask, you must believe and not doubt, because the one who doubts is like a wave of the sea, blown and tossed by the wind. That person should not expect to receive anything from the Lord. Such a person is double-minded and unstable in all they do.
JAMES 1:5–8 NIV

I will therefore that men pray every where, lifting up holy hands, without wrath and doubting.
1 TIMOTHY 2:8 KJV

*Let me, O my God, stifle forever in my heart, every thought that would tempt me to doubt thy goodness.*
FRANCOIS FENELON

# 20

## Dreams

Has God put a dream in your heart? Has some vision gripped your imagination? Do you feel God's calling on your life?

A dream is not necessarily the same as ambition. You can be ambitious to succeed in business to earn a good income, even though business is not your main passion. Your dream is what you'd pursue if money were no concern. It is your life goal.

A lot of people tinker with their dream in their spare hours and only engage in it full-time when they retire. Other people feel compelled to follow it in the middle of life, despite the financial hardships.

Surprisingly, many people know what their calling in life is but feel inadequate to fulfill it, and so resist it. Moses and Gideon did that.

A calling is often in the same area as your God-given talents—but not always. Also, you need to make sure that your aspirations are what God wants for your life.

Do that and you're ready to follow your dream.

By faith Noah, being warned by God concerning events as yet unseen, in reverent fear constructed an ark for the saving of his household.
HEBREWS 11:7 ESV

Abraham had faith and obeyed God. He was told to go to the land that God had said would be his, and he left for a country he had never seen. Because Abraham had faith, he lived as a stranger in the promised land.
HEBREWS 11:8–9 CEV

The king said to me, "What is it you want?" Then I prayed to the
God of heaven, and I answered the king, "If it pleases the king
and if your servant has found favor in his sight, let him send me
to the city in Judah where my ancestors are buried so that I
can rebuild it."
NEHEMIAH 2:4–5 NIV

*Resolve to pursue the dream God put in your heart. This involves
coming to the place where you declare, "Now is the time.
This is the place. I am the person."*
STEVE AND JANIE SJOGREN

This is a trustworthy saying: "If someone aspires to be an elder,
he desires an honorable position."
1 TIMOTHY 3:1 NLT

Then Moses said to the Israelites, "See, the LORD has chosen
Bezalel son of Uri, the son of Hur, of the tribe of Judah, and
he has filled him with the Spirit of God, with wisdom, with
understanding, with knowledge and with all kinds of skills—
to make artistic designs for work in gold, silver and bronze."
EXODUS 35:30–32 TNIV

*All Christians are called to develop God-given talents,
to make the most of their lives, to develop to the fullest their
God-given powers and capacities.*
HENRY BLACKABY

The aspirations of good people end in celebration;
the ambitions of bad people crash.
PROVERBS 10:28 MSG

Do you think you can mess with the dreams of the poor?
You can't, for God makes their dreams come true.
PSALM 14:5 MSG

*The question is not can you dream,*
*but do you have the courage to act on it?*
FRANKLIN JENTEZEN

Are you so foolish? After beginning by means of the Spirit,
are you now trying to finish by means of the flesh?
GALATIANS 3:3 NIV

Now when he was forty years old, it came into his heart to
visit his brethren, the children of Israel. And seeing one of them
suffer wrong, he defended and avenged him who was oppressed,
and struck down the Egyptian. For he supposed that his brethren
would have understood that God would deliver them by his hand,
but they did not understand.
ACTS 7:23–25 NKJV

*Anything we feel passionate about we can also overdo.*
PATRICK MORLEY

# 21

## Emotions

There's an unwritten code that men are supposed to be tough. . . all the time. Men don't show their emotions. And men don't cry.

The result has been generations of men who didn't emote or who felt weak when they did. So they kept it all inside. Things are changing in recent years with men encouraged—mostly by their wives—to show their sensitive sides.

The truth is, God built a wide range of emotions into our psyche and intended us to express them. It's simply not healthy to keep everything bottled up inside.

On the other hand, there are times when it's wise to maintain control over our emotions and not be carried away with them, or base important decisions on them.

Fear, for example, is a valid emotion—it keeps us out of danger—but many times we must master our fears and proceed regardless. The same is true for anger and sorrow.

Nevertheless, there is a time and a place for every emotion.

There is a time for everything. There's a time for everything that is done on earth. . . . There is a time to cry. And there's a time to laugh. There is a time to be sad. And there's a time to dance.
ECCLESIASTES 3:1, 4 NIrV

Our mouths were filled with laughter, our tongues with songs of joy. Then it was said among the nations, "The LORD has done great things for them."
PSALM 126:2 NIV

"Be angry, and do not sin": do not let the sun
go down on your wrath.
EPHESIANS 4:26 NKJV

Clean up your lives, you sinners. Purify your hearts, you people who can't make up your mind. Be sad and sorry and weep. Stop laughing and start crying. Be gloomy instead of glad.
JAMES 4:8–9 CEV

*One of the greatest gifts we are given are our emotions;*
*we need not fear our emotions.*
RICH HURST

[Jacob] approached his brother, bowed seven times, honoring his brother. But Esau ran up and embraced him, held him tight and kissed him. And they both wept.
GENESIS 33:4 MSG

Then Joseph looked at his brother Benjamin, the son of his own mother. . . . Then Joseph hurried from the room because he was overcome with emotion for his brother. He went into his private room, where he broke down and wept.
GENESIS 43:29–30 NLT

The seed cast in the gravel—this is the person who hears and instantly responds with enthusiasm. But there is no soil of character, and so when the emotions wear off and some difficulty arrives, there is nothing to show for it.
MATTHEW 13:20 MSG

*We have little control over our emotions but*
*tremendous control over our actions*
J. ALLAN PETERSEN

A sound mind makes for a robust body, but runaway emotions corrode the bones.
PROVERBS 14:30 MSG

A fool expresses all his emotions, but a wise person controls them.
PROVERBS 29:11 GW

Then God's peace, which goes beyond anything we can imagine, will guard your thoughts and emotions through Christ Jesus.
PHILIPPIANS 4:7 GW

*Anxiety, anger, and despair are infectious. Model emotional control.*
MARY PIPHER

# 22

## Eternal Life

Some people are enjoying "the good life" right now, and are soaking in its comforts and pleasures. They're quite satisfied by what this world has to offer.

Most of us, however, are weary of the hardships, injustices, pain, and sorrows of this life, and don't wish it to continue without end. On the other hand, we recoil at the thought of life ending permanently. We want to live on.

God reconciles these two opposing desires in an endless life in heaven where there is no more pain, nor sorrow, nor crying—an eternal reunion with God and loved ones in a paradise where all wrongs are made right and all good deeds rewarded.

We are sinful by nature, however, and don't deserve such a wonderful eternal life.

That's why God sent His Son, Jesus, to die for our sins. When we believe in Jesus and surrender our lives to Him, God adopts us as His sons and daughters, throws open heaven's doors, and invites us in.

For God loved the world so much that he gave his one and only Son, so that everyone who believes in him will not perish but have eternal life.
JOHN 3:16 NLT

Very truly I tell you, whoever hears my word and believes him who sent me has eternal life and will not be judged but has crossed over from death to life.
JOHN 5:24 NIV

God has shown us his love by sending his only Son into the world so that we could have life through him.
1 JOHN 4:9 GW

*Eternity to the godly is a day that has no sunset;*
*eternity to the wicked is a night that has no sunrise.*
THOMAS WATSON

Blessed is the man who endures temptation; for when he has been approved, he will receive the crown of life which the Lord has promised to those who love Him.
JAMES 1:12 NKJV

Let the person who has ears listen to what the Spirit says to the churches. I will give the privilege of eating from the tree of life, which stands in the paradise of God, to everyone who wins the victory.
REVELATION 2:7 GW

I say to you that many will come from the east and the west, and will take their places at the feast with Abraham, Isaac and Jacob in the kingdom of heaven.
MATTHEW 8:11 NIV

I'll give authority over the nations to all who overcome and who carry out my plans to the end.
REVELATION 2:26 NIrV

*Nothing can separate you from God's love, absolutely nothing.*
*God is enough for time, God is enough for eternity. God is enough!*
HANNAH WHITALL SMITH

God will reward each of us for what we have done. He will give eternal life to everyone who has patiently done what is good in the hope of receiving glory, honor, and life that lasts forever.
ROMANS 2:6–7 CEV

For you have been born again, but not to a life that will quickly end. Your new life will last forever because it comes from the eternal, living word of God.

1 PETER 1:23 NLT

But as it is written, Eye hath not seen, nor ear heard, neither have entered into the heart of man, the things which God hath prepared for them that love him.

1 CORINTHIANS 2:9 KJV

So "they are in front of the throne of God. They serve him day and night in his temple. The One who sits on the throne will spread his tent over them. Never again will they be hungry. Never again will they be thirsty. The sun will not beat down on them. The heat of the desert will not harm them. The Lamb, who is at the center of the area around the throne, will be their shepherd. He will lead them to springs of living water. And God will wipe away every tear from their eyes."

REVELATION 7:15–17 NIrV

*The best we can hope for in this life is a knothole peek at the shining realities ahead. Yet a glimpse is enough.*

JONI EARECKSON TADA

And God shall wipe away all tears from their eyes; and there shall be no more death, neither sorrow, nor crying, neither shall there be any more pain: for the former things are passed away.

REVELATION 21:4 KJV

*Lord, Your Word has given me a vision of eternity, and the Spirit speaks of its certainty in my heart. Let those who doubt never turn me from it.*

# 23

*Evil*

There is such a thing as evil—despite what some people say. You only have to turn on the television or browse the news on the Internet to realize that human beings are capable of great wickedness.

There is a spiritual dimension as well, and while the angels that inhabit it are dedicated to good, the fallen angels have given themselves over to doing evil.

We pray for God to protect us from evil—accidents, sicknesses, and attacks—and He has promised to do that. When He allows bad things to happen, however, it is often because He intends to bring good out of evil in the end.

We should also pray for God to keep us from thinking, speaking, and doing evil.

We must not deceive ourselves into thinking that because "we're not evil," that we're incapable of doing wrong. After all, the Bible warns Christians, "Repay no one evil for evil."

We must continually choose good and turn from evil every day.

You are not a God who delights in wickedness;
evil may not dwell with you.
PSALM 5:4 ESV

For our struggle is not against flesh and blood, but against the rulers, against the powers, against the world forces of this darkness, against the spiritual forces of wickedness in the heavenly places.
EPHESIANS 6:12 NASB

Repay no one evil for evil. Have regard for good things in the sight of all men.
ROMANS 12:17 NKJV

Good people bring good things out of their hearts, but evil people bring evil things out of their hearts. I promise you that on the day of judgment, everyone will have to account for every careless word they have spoken.
MATTHEW 12:35–36 CEV

> *Evil is real. But the problem of evil has ultimately one source: our rebellion against God's holiness.*
> RAVI ZACHARIAS AND KEVIN JOHNSON

Turn your back on evil, work for the good and don't quit.
PSALM 37:27 MSG

Keep your tongue from evil and your lips from speaking deceit. Depart from evil and do good; seek peace and pursue it.
PSALM 34:13–14 NASB

Put everything to the test. Accept what is good and don't have anything to do with evil.
1 THESSALONIANS 5:21–22 CEV

> *He who passively accepts evil is as much involved in it as he who helps to perpetrate it.*
> MARTIN LUTHER KING JR.

For you have made the LORD, my refuge, even the Most High, your dwelling place. No evil will befall you, nor will any plague come near your tent.
PSALM 91:9–10 NASB

Even though I walk through the darkest valley, I will fear no evil, for you are with me; your rod and your staff, they comfort me.
PSALM 23:4 NIV

The Lord will keep you from all evil; he will keep your life. The Lord will keep your going out and your coming in from this time forth and forevermore.
Psalm 121:7–8 ESV

> *God judged it better to bring good out of evil*
> *than to suffer no evil to exist.*
> Saint Augustine

But as for you, you meant evil against me; but God meant it for good, in order to bring it about as it is this day, to save many people alive.
Genesis 50:20 NKJV

# 24

## Exercise

Some of us have mistaken views about exercise because the four-hundred-year-old King James Bible states that "bodily exercise profiteth little" (1 Timothy 4:8). However, the New King James Version more clearly says: "bodily exercise profits a little."

The point Paul was making was that while there are benefits to physical exercise, there are far more benefits to spiritual exercise.

We know that a certain amount of exercise is needed to keep our physical bodies in shape and good health—whether it is workouts in the gym, jogging, or simply walking.

Many of us, however, avoid spiritual exercises for the same reason we avoid physical exercise: we're too busy, too lazy, find it boring, or don't understand its importance.

Exercising spiritually is work. It takes an effort of will to deny ourselves, carry our cross daily, and walk that extra mile with others. But if we exercise our spirits, we'll be in good shape and be able to stay in the race.

Exercise yourself toward godliness. For bodily exercise profits a little, but godliness is profitable for all things, having promise of the life that now is and of that which is to come.
1 TIMOTHY 4:7–8 NKJV

> *Bodily vigor is good, and vigor of intellect is even better,*
> *but far above both is character.*
> THEODORE ROOSEVELT

In them hath he set a tabernacle for the sun,
which. . .rejoiceth as a strong man to run a race.
PSALM 19:4–5 KJV

But Joab replied, "My son, why do you want to go? You don't have any news that will bring you a reward." He said, "Come what may, I want to run." So Joab said, "Run!"
2 SAMUEL 18:22–23 NIV

We went on ahead to the ship and sailed for Assos, where we were going to take Paul aboard. He had made this arrangement because he was going there on foot.
ACTS 20:13 NIV

*Look, my feet hurt some mornings, and my body is less forgiving when I exercise more than I am used to. But I love my life more, and me more.*
ANNE LAMOTT

The glory of young men is their strength, and the honor of old men is their gray hair.
PROVERBS 20:29 NASB

Moses was one hundred twenty years old when he died. His eyes were not weak, and he was still strong.
DEUTERONOMY 34:7 NCV

And now, behold, I am this day eighty-five years old. I am still as strong today as I was in the day that Moses sent me; my strength now is as my strength was then, for war and for going and coming.
JOSHUA 14:10–11 ESV

*If a man wins God's race, it doesn't matter where else he loses. If a man loses God's race, it matters not where else he may win.*
STEVEN LAWSON

Strip down, start running—and never quit! No extra spiritual fat, no parasitic sins. Keep your eyes on Jesus, who both began and finished this race we're in.

HEBREWS 12:1–2 MSG

So I strive always to keep my conscience clear before God and man.

ACTS 24:16 NIV

Don't you realize that in a race everyone runs, but only one person gets the prize? So run to win! All athletes are disciplined in their training. They do it to win a prize that will fade away, but we do it for an eternal prize.

1 CORINTHIANS 9:24–25 NLT

# 25

## Faiture

Despite putting forth our best efforts and praying for God to bless us, we don't succeed in every endeavor. We all experience failure at times.

Acknowledging that we've failed is difficult. Understanding why we failed isn't easy either, but if we are to go on and not repeat our mistakes, we must honestly assess what we did wrong and learn the lessons.

Sometimes we fail because of sin in our lives. Sometimes it's our inexperience or wrong attitudes. Sometimes we fall because we presume (mistakenly, as it turns out) that God is bound to bless our venture, so we overextend ourselves.

Failure is not always negative. Sometimes we need to fail in one area to make us willing to look elsewhere and try something new. Or sometimes the lessons learned are so valuable that failing was a necessary part of our journey.

Sometimes failure is not really failure at all—not in God's eyes. Hardships are often a natural result of faithfully living as a Christian.

Because they rebelled against the words of God, and despised the counsel of the Most High, therefore He brought down their heart with labor.
PSALM 107:11–12 NKJV

Stay away from her! Don't go near the door of her house! If you do, you will lose your honor and will lose to merciless people all you have achieved. Strangers will consume your wealth, and someone else will enjoy the fruit of your labor.
PROVERBS 5:8–10 NLT

*Calamity is the perfect glass wherein we truly see and know ourselves.*
WILLIAM D'AVENANT

"You expected much, but see, it turned out to be little. What you brought home, I blew away. Why?" declares the LORD Almighty. "Because of my house, which remains a ruin, while each of you is busy with his own house."
HAGGAI 1:9 TNIV

If you don't confess your sins, you will be a failure. But God will be merciful if you confess your sins and give them up.
PROVERBS 28:13 CEV

Trust in your wealth, and you will be a failure, but God's people will prosper like healthy plants.
PROVERBS 11:28 CEV

*If a dream that God has given you dies, it may be that God wants to see what's more important to you. The dream or Him.*
PHIL VISCHER

Now in my prosperity I said, "I shall never be moved." LORD, by Your favor You have made my mountain stand strong; You hid Your face, and I was troubled.
PSALM 30:6–7 NKJV

I returned, and saw under the sun, that the race is not to the swift, nor the battle to the strong, neither yet bread to the wise, nor yet riches to men of understanding, nor yet favour to men of skill; but time and chance happeneth to them all.
ECCLESIASTES 9:11 KJV

Enjoy prosperity while you can, but when hard times strike, realize that both come from God. Remember that nothing is certain in this life.

ECCLESIASTES 7:14 NLT

*No matter how well we live our Christian life, circumstances will not always turn out the way we want.*

TULLIAN TCHIVIDJIAN

The steps of a good man are ordered by the LORD, and He delights in his way. Though he fall, he shall not be utterly cast down; for the LORD upholds him with His hand.

PSALM 37:23–24 NKJV

Therefore, my beloved brethren, be ye stedfast, unmoveable, always abounding in the work of the Lord, forasmuch as ye know that your labour is not in vain in the Lord.

1 CORINTHIANS 15:58 KJV

"I have toiled in vain, I have spent My strength for nothing and vanity; yet surely the justice due to Me is with the LORD, and My reward with My God."

ISAIAH 49:4 NASB

*Our perception of success and failure may, in fact be inaccurate. . . perhaps the almighty God has chosen to work through us without letting us know. We may find out years later that what we saw as failure was actually God's success.*

ALICE FRYLING

# 26

## Fatherhood

Children are a natural result of the love between a man and his wife, and God has given us a natural instinct to love our own. Or if we adopt children, it is a choice made out of love.

A newborn baby brings great joy and satisfaction to a father's heart, but we quickly learn that caring for that child is a serious responsibility.

All parents, consistently or not, seek to instill their beliefs and values in their children. As Christian fathers, we are commanded to not only set a godly example, but to make a conscious effort to teach them about the Lord.

We are also instructed to discipline them when they need it—firmly but not harshly. Correction and setting boundaries are essential parts of child rearing.

Our children will know by the way we interact with them how much we love them. And it's important that they know, because as fathers we are a crucially important model of their Father in heaven.

Children's children are the crown of old men; and the glory of children are their fathers.
PROVERBS 17:6 KJV

These commandments that I give you today are to be on your hearts. Impress them on your children. Talk about them when you sit at home and when you walk along the road, when you lie down and when you get up.
DEUTERONOMY 6:6–7 NIV

> *The children you and I can influence are more open to the things of the Spirit than adults often realize.*
> JACK W. HAYFORD

My child, listen to your father's teaching and do not forget
your mother's advice.
PROVERBS 1:8 NCV

A fool rejects his father's discipline, but he who regards
reproof is sensible.
PROVERBS 15:5 NASB

A refusal to correct is a refusal to love;
love your children by disciplining them.
PROVERBS 13:24 MSG

> *Good behavior is convenient for us as parents,*
> *but we must not confuse it with a will submitted to God.*
> CHRISTINE M. FIELD

Don't fail to correct your children. You won't kill them by being
firm, and it may even save their lives.
PROVERBS 23:13–14 CEV

Fathers, do not exasperate your children; instead, bring them up
in the training and instruction of the Lord.
EPHESIANS 6:4 TNIV

Fathers, do not provoke your children,
lest they become discouraged.
COLOSSIANS 3:21 NKJV

> *Children have more need of example than criticism.*
> CAROL KUYKENDALL

He must manage his own family well and see that his children obey him, and he must do so in a manner worthy of full respect. (If anyone does not know how to manage his own family, how can he take care of God's church?)

1 TIMOTHY 3:4–5 NIV

Since we respected our earthly fathers who disciplined us, shouldn't we submit even more to the discipline of the Father of our spirits, and live forever? For our earthly fathers disciplined us for a few years, doing the best they knew how. But God's discipline is always good for us, so that we might share in his holiness.

HEBREWS 12:9–10 NLT

*It is time we stand up for what we believe and teach those eternal truths to our children.*

JAMES DOBSON

# 27

*Fear*

The Bible describes two kinds of fear: first, there's the fear of, or reverence for, God. This is a positive thing. "The fear of the Lord is pure" (Psalm 19:9 NIV). It draws us closer to Him in respect and love.

Then there's the fear of man. This is a negative thing. "Fearing people is a dangerous trap" (Proverbs 29:25 NLT). This is the paralyzing fear that focuses on all the ways that people could hurt us. Such fear shows our lack of trust in God.

However, even great Bible heroes experienced anxious fear. David did, time and again. But rather than letting it overcome him, he fell to his knees and cried out to God for protection and peace of mind.

David admitted that he was fearful, but declared to the Lord, "But when I am afraid, I will put my trust in you" (Psalm 56:3 NLT). God then replaced his fear with courage.

He can do the same thing for us today.

Oh, that [the Hebrews] had such a heart in them that they would fear Me and always keep all My commandments, that it might be well with them and with their children forever!
DEUTERONOMY 5:29 NKJV

What does the Lord your God require of you, but to fear the Lord your God, to walk in all His ways and to love Him, to serve the Lord your God with all your heart and with all your soul, and to keep. . .His statutes which I command you today for your good?
DEUTERONOMY 10:12–13 NKJV

I sought the Lord, and He heard me, and delivered me from all my fears.
PSALM 34:4 NKJV

*Are you facing fear today? . . . At times all of us experience fear.*
*But don't allow fear to keep you from being used by God. He has kept*
*you thus far; trust Him for the rest of the way.*
WOODROW KROLL

Yea, though I walk through the valley of the shadow of death,
I will fear no evil: for thou art with me; thy rod and thy staff
they comfort me.
PSALM 23:4 KJV

God is our refuge and strength, always ready to help in times
of trouble. So we will not fear when earthquakes come and the
mountains crumble into the sea. Let the oceans roar and foam.
Let the mountains tremble as the waters surge!
PSALM 46:1–3 NLT

*Fear is born of Satan, and if we would only take time to think a*
*moment we would see that everything Satan says*
*is founded upon a falsehood.*
A. B. SIMPSON

Many. . .are pursuing and attacking me, but even when I am
afraid, I keep on trusting you. I praise your promises! I trust you
and am not afraid. No one can harm me.
PSALM 56:2–4 CEV

Though a host encamp against me, my heart will not fear;
though war arise against me, in spite of this I shall be confident.
PSALM 27:3 NASB

*Faith, which is trust, and fear are opposite poles. If a man has the one,*
*he can scarcely have the other in vigorous operation.*
ALEXANDER MACLAREN

God has said, "Never will I leave you; never will I forsake you." So we say with confidence, "The Lord is my helper; I will not be afraid. What can mere mortals do to me?"
HEBREWS 13:5–6 NIV

There is no fear in love; but perfect love casts out fear, because fear involves punishment, and the one who fears is not perfected in love.
1 JOHN 4:18 NASB

For God has not given us a spirit of fear, but of power and of love and of a sound mind.
2 TIMOTHY 1:7 NKJV

# 28

*Finances*

Cash may be cold and hard, but financial matters are not un-spiritual. Rather, how we handle money is one of the clearest measures of our love for God.

The Bible talks a great deal about money. And while the Lord warns us not to set our heart on riches, He also stresses the importance of working hard to earn a living to provide for our families.

And if He blesses us with wealth, that's a good thing.

The Bible repeatedly teaches the importance of giving generously—both to God's work and to the needy. But there is more to good money management than giving.

The Scriptures also promote savings and investments, underscores the need for financial planning, and reminds us to pay our taxes.

Through it all we must keep one principle in mind: our money is not actually "ours." It belongs to God—just as we ourselves are God's possessions. We are simply stewards of the finances God has entrusted to our care.

And it is a good thing to receive wealth from God and the good health to enjoy it. To enjoy your work and accept your lot in life—this is indeed a gift from God.
ECCLESIASTES 5:19 NLT

*Enormous fortunes have been built on small amounts of money faithfully invested over time. The same is true of relationships.*
NANCY COBB AND CONNIE GRIGSBY

Why then didn't you put my money on deposit, so that when I came back, I could have collected it with interest?
LUKE 19:23 NIV

The man knew what each servant could do. So he handed five thousand coins to the first servant, two thousand to the second, and one thousand to the third. Then he left the country. As soon as the man had gone, the servant with the five thousand coins used them to earn five thousand more.

MATTHEW 25:15–16 CEV

Precious treasure and oil are in a wise man's dwelling, but a foolish man devours it.

PROVERBS 21:20 ESV

Whoever loves pleasure will become poor; whoever loves wine and olive oil will never be rich.

PROVERBS 21:17 NIV

> *The essence of a financial plan is to determine the best way, as a manager, to handle God's money that He has entrusted to you.*
> DEBORAH SMITH PEGUES

You people who don't want to work, think about the ant! Consider its ways and be wise! It has no commander. It has no leader or ruler. But it stores up its food in summer. It gathers its food at harvest time.

PROVERBS 6:6–8 NIrV

By wisdom a house is built, and by understanding it is established; and by knowledge the rooms are filled with all precious and pleasant riches.

PROVERBS 24:3–4 NASB

> *Trust not to the omnipotency of gold,*
> *and say not unto it thou art my confidence.*
> THOMAS BROWN

But don't begin until you count the cost. For who would begin construction of a building without first calculating the cost to see if there is enough money to finish it?
LUKE 14:28 NLT

The rich ruleth over the poor, and the borrower is servant to the lender.
PROVERBS 22:7 KJV

Do not wear yourself out to get rich;
do not trust your own cleverness.
PROVERBS 23:4 NIV

Honor the LORD with your wealth, with the firstfruits of all your crops; then your barns will be filled to overflowing, and your vats will brim over with new wine.
PROVERBS 3:9–10 NIV

*God deserves first place in our lives. That means our finances, too. Giving a portion to God first reflects an attitude that God has priority in your family finances.*
BRUCE BICKEL AND STAN JANTZ

Command those who are rich in this present age not to be haughty, nor to trust in uncertain riches but in the living God, who gives us richly all things to enjoy. Let them do good, that they be rich in good works, ready to give, willing to share.
1 TIMOTHY 6:17–18 NKJV

# 29

## Following God

Following God means literally that: to follow in His footsteps as we walk through life. John tells us how to follow God's Son, Jesus, saying: "He who says he abides in Him ought. . .to walk just as He walked" (1 John 2:6 NKJV).

"Following God" is another term for "being a disciple." It entails believing in God, loving Him, faithfully sticking to Him, and—very importantly—obeying Him.

Jesus said that if we truly love Him, we would obey His commands. Following God means disciplining ourselves to live a life that emulates our Teacher, to die to our old desires and habits, and live our lives according to what He said.

Jesus knew that following Him would be rough at times. He therefore warned us that we'd need to deny ourselves many things, exercise self-control, and think more about others and less about ourselves, if we are to be His disciples.

To truly follow God costs us, but the rewards are great.

And now, Israel, what does the LORD your God ask of you but to fear the LORD your God, to walk in obedience to him, to love him, to serve the LORD your God with all your heart and with all your soul, and to observe the LORD's commands and decrees that I am giving you today for your own good?
DEUTERONOMY 10:12–13 NIV

And thou shalt love the Lord thy God with all thy heart, and with all thy soul, and with all thy mind, and with all thy strength: this is the first commandment.
MARK 12:30 KJV

You shall follow the LORD your God and fear Him; and you shall
keep His commandments, listen to His voice, serve Him,
and cling to Him.
DEUTERONOMY 13:4 NASB

*The correct perspective is to see following Christ not only as the
necessity it is, but as the fulfillment of the highest human
possibilities and as life on the highest plane.*
DALLAS WILLARD

Then Jesus spoke to them again, saying, "I am the light of the
world. He who follows Me shall not walk in darkness,
but have the light of life."
JOHN 8:12 NKJV

And he said to them all, If any man will come after me, let him
deny himself, and take up his cross daily, and follow me. For
whosoever will save his life shall lose it: but whosoever will lose
his life for my sake, the same shall save it.
LUKE 9:23–24 KJV

You have accepted Christ Jesus as your Lord.
Now keep on following him.
COLOSSIANS 2:6 CEV

*The rule that governs my life is this: Anything that dims my vision of
Christ, or takes away my taste for Bible study, or cramps my prayer
life, or makes Christian work difficult, is wrong for me, and I must,
as a Christian, turn away from it.*
J. WILBUR CHAPMAN

So Jesus said to those Jews who believed in him, "If you live by what I say, you are truly my disciples. You will know the truth, and the truth will set you free."
JOHN 8:31–32 GW

But whoever keeps His word, truly the love of God is perfected in him. By this we know that we are in Him. He who says he abides in Him ought himself also to walk just as He walked.
1 JOHN 2:5–6 NKJV

So I say, walk by the Spirit, and you will not gratify the desires of the flesh.
GALATIANS 5:16 NIV

> *The Christian ideal has not been tried and found wanting.*
> *It has been found difficult and left untried.*
> G. K. CHESTERTON

But now that you have come to know God, or rather to be known by God, how can you turn back again to the weak and worthless elementary principles of the world, whose slaves you want to be once more?
GALATIANS 4:9 ESV

If someone says, "I love God," and hates his brother, he is a liar; for he who does not love his brother whom he has seen, how can he love God whom he has not seen? And this commandment we have from Him: that he who loves God must love his brother also.
1 JOHN 4:20–21 NKJV

> *One of the rewards of following Christ is the simplicity*
> *and wonder it brings to life.*
> JOSEPH M. STOWELL

# 30

*Forgiveness*

A true proverb states: "To err is human; to forgive is divine." We once lived in a state of sin and rebellion against God, and deserved to be punished. But God had no joy in seeing us perish. He loved us and wanted to restore a relationship between us.

Therefore, moved with tender mercy, God made a way to bring us into His arms. He sent His Son, Jesus, to take our punishment upon Himself. When we repented of our sins and believed in Jesus, God forgave our many sins.

And He continues to forgive us when we stumble in our Christian walk.

God has not only been extremely tenderhearted toward us, but to others as well. He therefore commands us to be loving and compassionate to others—just as He is. When a relationship has been marred by an offense, He wants us to forgive—just as He does.

Relationships are ruined by bitterness and grudges. They are restored by compassion and forgiveness.

Who is a God like you, who pardons sin and forgives the transgression of the remnant of his inheritance? You do not stay angry forever but delight to show mercy. You will again have compassion on us; you will tread our sins underfoot and hurl all our iniquities into the depths of the sea.
Micah 7:18–19 NIV

The Lord is slow to anger, abounding in love
and forgiving sin and rebellion.
Numbers 14:18 TNIV

You are a forgiving God, gracious and compassionate,
slow to anger and abounding in love.
NEHEMIAH 9:17 NIV

*God forgave us without any merit on our part; therefore we must
forgive others, whether or not we think they merit it.*
LEHMAN STRAUSS

Bless the LORD, O my soul, and forget not all His benefits:
who forgives all your iniquities, who heals all your diseases,
who redeems your life from destruction, who crowns you with
lovingkindness and tender mercies.
PSALM 103:2–4 NKJV

Be kind and tender to one another. Forgive each other,
just as God forgave you because of what Christ has done.
EPHESIANS 4:32 NIrV

If you forgive other people when they sin against you, your
heavenly Father will also forgive you. But if you do not forgive
others their sins, your Father will not forgive your sins.
MATTHEW 6:14–15 NIV

*We need not climb up into heaven to see whether our sins are forgiven:
let us look into our hearts, and see if we can forgive others.
If we can, we need not doubt but God has forgiven us.*
THOMAS WATSON

Then Peter came to him and asked, "Lord, how often should I
forgive someone who sins against me? Seven times?" "No, not
seven times," Jesus replied, "but seventy times seven!"
MATTHEW 18:21–22 NLT

And when you stand praying, if you hold anything against anyone, forgive them, so that your Father in heaven may forgive you your sins.

MARK 11:25 NIV

Take heed to yourselves. If your brother sins against you, rebuke him; and if he repents, forgive him. And if he sins against you seven times in a day, and seven times in a day returns to you, saying, "I repent," you shall forgive him.

LUKE 17:3–4 NKJV

> *Forgiveness is an act of the will, and the will can function regardless of the temperature of the heart.*
>
> CORRIE TEN BOOM

When people sin, you should forgive and comfort them, so they won't give up in despair. You should make them sure of your love for them.

2 CORINTHIANS 2:7–8 CEV

# 31

## God's Discipline

When you first became a Christian, perhaps you believed that from then on you'd be happy all the time—that is, 'til you experienced frustrations, sorrow, and grief.

Perhaps you were taught that if you obeyed God and gave faithfully to the Church, that He'd be certain to always bless your health and finances. But sickness and financial problems shook that notion to its core.

To make matters worse, while you were suffering hardship and grief, you happened to notice that your worldly neighbors were prospering and happy.

What happened? Was God punishing you for sin or lack of faith?

Possibly. But more likely God was putting you through the fires to purify you. God chastens (disciplines) all His children. It's proof that you belong to Him and that He loves you.

Discipline isn't easy to endure—and perhaps you'd rather not if you had a choice—but God cares too much about you to leave you the way you are. He wants you to grow spiritually.

For I envied the proud when I saw them prosper despite their wickedness. They seem to live such painless lives; their bodies are so healthy and strong. They don't have troubles like other people; they're not plagued with problems like everyone else.
PSALM 73:3–5 NLT

> *God disciplines those who He loves,*
> *but He does not stop loving those He disciplines.*
> COLIN S. SMITH

And have you completely forgotten this word of encouragement that addresses you as a father addresses his son? It says, "My son, do not make light of the Lord's discipline, and do not lose heart when he rebukes you, because the Lord disciplines the one he loves, and he chastens everyone he accepts as his son." Endure hardship as discipline; God is treating you as his children. For what children are not disciplined by their father? If you are not disciplined—and everyone undergoes discipline—then you are not legitimate, not true sons and daughters at all.
HEBREWS 12:5–8 NIV

All discipline for the moment seems not to be joyful, but sorrowful; yet to those who have been trained by it, afterwards it yields the peaceful fruit of righteousness.
HEBREWS 12:11 NASB

Know then in your heart that as a man disciplines his son, so the LORD your God disciplines you.
DEUTERONOMY 8:5 NIV

O LORD, blessed is the person whom you discipline and instruct from your teachings.
PSALM 94:12 GW

*If you are a child of God whose heart's desire is to see God glorified through you, adversity will not put you down for the count.*
CHARLES STANLEY

LORD, in trouble they have visited You, they poured out a prayer when Your chastening was upon them.
ISAIAH 26:16 NKJV

"For has anyone said to God, 'I have borne punishment; I will not offend any more; teach me what I do not see [in regard to how I have sinned]; if I have done iniquity, I will do it no more'?"

JOB 34:31–32 ESV

Consider it a sheer gift, friends, when tests and challenges come at you from all sides. You know that under pressure, your faith-life is forced into the open and shows its true colors. So don't try to get out of anything prematurely. Let it do its work so you become mature and well-developed, not deficient in any way.

JAMES 1:2–3 MSG

*There are certain things in this life that God can reveal to us only in the midst of adversity. There are hidden places deep in our souls He can reach only through our suffering.*

MARY NELSON

# 32
## God's Love

From the Old Testament to the New, the Bible writers tell us how great God's love is and how He lavishes it upon us, His children. Long after we would have given up loving someone, God still loves. He never stops.

"How can God be so loving?" we ask. "In fact, why would He be?" The answer is found in 1 John 4:16, which states: "God is love" (NIV). It is His very nature to love.

We must get this truth firmly fixed in our minds. Until we do, we'll have a lopsided concept of what God is like—and therefore won't understand how He relates to us.

As a result, we'll misjudge His motives when He allows us to experience hardships: we'll think He's unfair and become bitter and distant—or think He's judging us and become confused and discouraged.

Yes, God loves justice. Yes, God will punish the wicked. Yes, God is grieved by sin. But we must grasp how much God loves us!

Understand, therefore, that the LORD your God is indeed God. He is the faithful God who keeps his covenant for a thousand generations and lavishes his unfailing love on those who love him and obey his commands.
DEUTERONOMY 7:9 NLT

Thank GOD! He deserves your thanks. His love never quits. Thank the God of all gods, His love never quits. Thank the Lord of all lords. His love never quits.
PSALM 136:1–2 MSG

*The Cross is the ultimate evidence that there is no length the love of God will refuse to go in effecting reconciliation.*
R. KENT HUGHES

For God so loved the world that He gave His only begotten Son, that whoever believes in Him should not perish but have everlasting life.
JOHN 3:16 NKJV

This is how we know what love is:
Jesus Christ laid down his life for us.
1 JOHN 3:16 TNIV

This is love: not that we loved God, but that he loved us and sent his Son as an atoning sacrifice for our sins.
1 JOHN 4:10 NIV

*We keep asking, "Who am I that the Lord should love me?" Instead we ought to be asking, "Who are you, O my God, that you love me so much?"*
JOHN POWELL

The Father Himself loves you, because you have loved Me and have believed that I came forth from the Father.
JOHN 16:27 NASB

I will always trust in God's unfailing love.
PSALM 52:8 NLT

Nothing in all creation can separate us from God's love for us in Christ Jesus our Lord!
ROMANS 8:39 CEV

God's love has been poured out into our hearts through the Holy Spirit, who has been given to us. You see, at just the right time, when we were still powerless, Christ died for the ungodly. Very rarely will anyone die for a righteous person, though for a good person someone might possibly dare to die. But God demonstrates his own love for us in this: While we were still sinners, Christ died for us.
ROMANS 5:5–8 NIV

*If we comprehend what Christ has done for us, then surely out of gratitude we will strive to live "worthy" of such great love. We will strive for holiness not to make God love us but because He already does.*
PHILIP YANCEY

We have come to know and have believed the love which God has for us. God is love, and the one who abides in love abides in God, and God abides in him.
1 JOHN 4:16 NASB

Therefore be imitators of God as dear children. And walk in love, as Christ also has loved us and given Himself for us, an offering and a sacrifice to God for a sweet-smelling aroma.
EPHESIANS 5:1–3 NKJV

# 33
## God's Will

When we talk about God's will, we're referring to a specific behavior or event that God is intent on bringing about.

When it comes to God's overall will for our lives, the Bible gives very clear commands on how He wants us to live. He gives us straightforward rules to order our lives by.

We understand this. But what we often want to know is, "What is God's specific will for my life?" We want to know which career to pursue, who to marry, where to live, etc.

It can take quite a bit of prayer, thinking, researching, and counseling to determine God's will in personal matters, but we can rest assured, God does have a plan and will reveal it if we earnestly seek it.

The key is to be willing to set aside our own plans if God's will is different from ours. This won't be too difficult if we're already submitting ourselves to His overall, revealed will for our lives.

You must not have any other god but me.
EXODUS 20:3 NLT

And you must love the LORD your God with all your heart, all your soul, and all your strength.
DEUTERONOMY 6:5 NLT

Therefore, my dear friends, as you have always obeyed. . . continue to work out your salvation with fear and trembling, for it is God who works in you to will and to act in order to fulfill his good purpose.
PHILIPPIANS 2:12–13 NIV

*Proceed with much prayer, and your way will be made plain.*
JOHN WESLEY

*We discover the will of God by a sensitive application*
*of Scripture to our own lives.*
SINCLAIR FERGUSON

And do not be conformed to this world, but be transformed by
the renewing of your mind, so that you may prove what the will
of God is, that which is good and acceptable and perfect.
ROMANS 12:2 NASB

Be very careful, then, how you live—not as unwise but as wise,
making the most of every opportunity, because the days are evil.
Therefore do not be foolish, but understand what the Lord's will
is. Do not get drunk on wine, which leads to debauchery. Instead,
be filled with the Spirit.
EPHESIANS 5:15–18 NIV

*We must know that as His children, He's going to allow problems even*
*when we are in the centre of His will.*
SANDY EDMONSON

Even so it is not the will of your Father which is in heaven, that
one of these little ones should perish.
MATTHEW 18:14 KJV

Our Father in heaven, hallowed be your name, your kingdom
come, your will be done, on earth as it is in heaven.
MATTHEW 6:9–10 NIV

"Father, if You are willing, remove this cup from Me;
yet not My will, but Yours be done."
LUKE 22:42 NASB

# 34

## God's Word

God's words have tremendous power. At the very beginning in Genesis, God simply said, "Let there be light," and there was light. He continued to speak and His words brought the entire universe into existence.

When God spoke to prophets such as Moses, Jeremiah, and others, they recorded "the word of the Lord," and this growing collection of books became known as the Word of God. Today, God's Word means the entire Bible, from Genesis to Revelation.

Like His spoken word at Creation, God's written Word has great power. It teaches us how to be saved, gives us wisdom, guides us, convicts us of sin, and encourages us when we're down.

We are urged to read it, meditate on it, believe it, memorize it, and quote it.

Jesus is called the Word of God—"the Word made flesh." The Greek word *logos*—which meant the spoken word that governed the universe—was understood by the Jews to be referring to God Himself.

By the word of the LORD the heavens were made, and by the breath of His mouth all their host. . . . For He spoke, and it was done; He commanded, and it stood fast.
PSALM 33:6, 9 NASB

Forever, O LORD, your word is firmly fixed in the heavens.
PSALM 119.09 ESV

After he was raised from the dead, his disciples recalled what he had said. Then they believed the scripture and the words that Jesus had spoken.
JOHN 2:22 NIV

"All people are like grass, and all their glory is like the flowers of the field; the grass withers and the flowers fall, but the word of the Lord endures forever." And this is the word that was preached to you.
1 PETER 1:24–25 NIV

*Too often, we look to the Bible as our guidebook for daily living. Of course, that's fine and even biblical. However, this collection of books we call the Holy Bible is much more than a self-help book. The divine purpose of this book is to point us to the One and Only.*
RANDY HUNT

All Scripture is God-breathed and is useful for teaching, rebuking, correcting and training in righteousness, so that the servant of God may be thoroughly equipped for every good work.
2 TIMOTHY 3:16–17 NIV

*The Bible cannot be understood simply by study or talent; you must count only on the influence of the Holy Spirit.*
MARTIN LUTHER

Above all, you must realize that no prophecy in Scripture ever came from the prophet's own understanding, or from human initiative. No, those prophets were moved by the Holy Spirit, and they spoke from God.
2 PETER 1:20–21 NLT

So the Word became human and made his home among us. He was full of unfailing love and faithfulness. And we have seen his glory, the glory of the Father's one and only Son.
JOHN 1:14 NLT

Thy word is a lamp unto my feet, and a light unto my path.
PSALM 119:105 KJV

The Son is the radiance of God's glory and the exact representation of his being, sustaining all things by his powerful word. After he had provided purification for sins, he sat down at the right hand of the Majesty in heaven.
HEBREWS 1:3 NIV

For the word of the LORD is right and true; he is faithful in all he does.
PSALM 33:4 TNIV

> *Beware of reasoning about God's Word—obey it.*
> OSWALD CHAMBERS

For the word of God is alive and active. Sharper than any double-edged sword, it penetrates even to dividing soul and spirit, joints and marrow; it judges the thoughts and attitudes of the heart.
HEBREWS 4:12 TNIV

So get rid of all the filth and evil in your lives, and humbly accept the word God has planted in your hearts, for it has the power to save your souls. But don't just listen to God's word. You must do what it says. Otherwise, you are only fooling yourselves. For if you listen to the word and don't obey, it is like glancing at your face in a mirror.
JAMES 1:21–23 NLT

> *Defend the Bible? I would just as soon defend a lion.*
> *Just turn the Bible loose. It will defend itself.*
> CHARLES H. SPURGEON

I have written to you who are young in the faith because you are strong. God's word lives in your hearts, and you have won your battle with the evil one.
1 JOHN 2:14 NLT

# 35

*Hope*

We need hope or we simply can't go on. When we lose hope we feel like giving up. So what exactly is hope?

The pagans of Paul's day viewed hope as a feeble, desperate thing—nothing solid. Paul described them as "having no hope, and without God in the world" (Ephesians 2:12 KJV).

Today, though society recognizes the importance of hope, when people say, "Don't give up hope," they're only wishing that things might get better. Their assumptions aren't based on any certain, solid foundation.

A Christian's hope, however, is based on the power and the Word of God. We have hope for eternal life because God raised Jesus Christ from the dead—and will raise us as well.

We have hope in this life as well, because we know that God is good and loves us deeply. We can have an enduring trust in Him even when everything seems to be coming unraveled, and our plans go awry.

As Christians, we have good reason to hope.

Lead me by your truth and teach me, for you are the God who saves me. All day long I put my hope in you.
PSALM 25:5 NLT

No one who hopes in you will ever be put to shame, but shame will come on those who are treacherous without cause.
PSALM 25:3 NIV

For God alone, O my soul, wait in silence,
for my hope is from him.
PSALM 62:5 ESV

*As far as the Lord is concerned, the time to stand is in the darkest moment. It is when everything seems hopeless, when there appears no way out, when God alone can deliver.*

DAVID WILKERSON

Why, my soul, are you downcast? Why so disturbed within me?
Put your hope in God, for I will yet praise him,
my Savior and my God.
PSALM 42:11 NIV

Even when there was no reason for hope, Abraham kept hoping—believing that he would become the father of many nations. For God had said to him, "That's how many descendants you will have!"
ROMANS 4:18 NLT

Now faith is the substance of things hoped for,
the evidence of things not seen.
HEBREWS 11:1 NKJV

*If you have any hope, it comes from some faith in you. Hope, you may say, is a bud upon the plant of faith, a bud from the root of faith; the flower is joy and peace.*

GEORGE MACDONALD

And not only this, but also we ourselves, having the first fruits of the Spirit, even we ourselves groan within ourselves, waiting eagerly for our adoption as sons, the redemption of our body. For in hope we have been saved, but hope that is seen is not hope; for who hopes for what he already sees? But if we hope for what we do not see, with perseverance we wait eagerly for it.
ROMANS 8:23–25 NASB

*He that lives in hope danceth without music.*
GEORGE HERBERT

We boast in the hope of the glory of God. Not only so, but we also glory in our sufferings, because we know that suffering produces perseverance; perseverance, character; and character, hope. And hope does not put us to shame, because God's love has been poured out into our hearts through the Holy Spirit, who has been given to us.
ROMANS 5:2–5 NIV

Be joyful in hope, patient in affliction, faithful in prayer.
ROMANS 12:12 TNIV

Though He slay me, I will hope in Him.
JOB 13:15 NASB

# 36

## Integrity

Integrity means moral uprightness and honesty. A man who has integrity is uncorrupted. Our English word *integrity* comes from the same Latin root word as "whole." Someone who is said to be whole is sound through and through.

Honesty and uprightness are an integral part of who he is.

His values are not merely a superficial show, but have been wholly integrated into his being—and manifest themselves in everything that he does and says.

You can count on a man of integrity to treat you fairly and honestly. You can trust him to keep his word. He will do what he said he would do.

A man of integrity has a good reputation—and it is well deserved.

God knows, however, that we are weak, fallible men. We often come to Him anything but whole and uncorrupted. Fortunately for us, God is in the business of transforming lives. His Holy Spirit can renew us and build integrity where formerly we had none.

I know, my God, that you test the heart and are pleased with integrity.
1 CHRONICLES 29:17 NIV

Let the LORD judge the peoples. Vindicate me, LORD, according to my righteousness, according to my integrity, O Most High.
PSALM 7:8 NIV

*Integrity characterizes the entire person, not just part of him.*
*He is righteous and honest through and through.*
*He is not only that inside, but also in outer action.*
R. KENT HUGHES

Godliness guards the path of the blameless,
but the evil are misled by sin.
Proverbs 13:6 NLT

God can't stand deceivers, but oh how he relishes integrity.
Proverbs 11:20 MSG

> *Today, there are far too many men with reputation*
> *(what men say about you) and far too few men with integrity*
> *(what God knows about you).*
> Rick Scarborough

Then the Lord asked Satan, "Have you noticed my servant Job?
He is the finest man in all the earth. He is blameless—a man of
complete integrity. He fears God and stays away from evil. And
he has maintained his integrity, even though you urged me to
harm him without cause."
Job 2:3 NLT

Now if you walk before Me as your father David walked, in
integrity of heart and in uprightness, to do according to all that
I have commanded you, and if you keep My statutes and My
judgments, then I will establish the throne of your kingdom over
Israel forever, as I promised David your father, saying, "You shall
not fail to have a man on the throne of Israel."
1 Kings 9:4–5 NKJV

> *Integrity is keeping a commitment even after*
> *circumstances have changed.*
> David Jeremiah

May integrity and honesty protect me, for I put my hope in you.
Psalm 25:21 NLT

The integrity of the upright guides them, but the unfaithful are destroyed by their duplicity.

PROVERBS 11:3 NIV

By this I know that You are pleased with me, because my enemy does not shout in triumph over me. As for me, You uphold me in my integrity, and You set me in Your presence forever.

PSALM 41:11–12 NASB

In everything set them an example by doing what is good. In your teaching show integrity, seriousness and soundness of speech that cannot be condemned, so that those who oppose you may be ashamed because they have nothing bad to say about us.

TITUS 2:7–8 NIV

> *Integrity is a part of our character and is best known by three behaviors: telling the truth; keeping one's promises; taking responsibility for one's behavior.*
> ROSS CAMPBELL, MD

And then you need to keep a sharp eye out for competent men—men who fear God, men of integrity, men who are incorruptible—and appoint them as leaders over groups organized by the thousand, by the hundred, by fifty, and by ten.

EXODUS 18:21 MSG

# 37

## Joy

We normally think of joy as great, exuberant happiness in response to something tremendously good happening: we enjoy unexpected good fortune, a serious crisis has a happy ending, or we marry the woman of our dreams, etc.

The Bible often talks about this kind of joy. But it also talks about the kind of joy God gives us when we're in the middle of adversity—at a time when by all accounts, we'd be expected to be miserable or worried.

How is it actually humanly possible to have joy in times like that?

It's possible if we dwell close to God, if we're full of His Holy Spirit—because joy is a natural result of being in the presence of God. Where God dwells, there is joy.

We also know that God will work out a happy conclusion to our circumstances, so even though we're in the middle of trouble now, that knowledge gives us joy.

This is why the Bible constantly tells us to rejoice.

Splendor and majesty are before him;
strength and joy are in his dwelling place.
1 CHRONICLES 16:27 NIV

You will show me the way of life, granting me the joy of your presence and the pleasures of living with you forever.
PSALM 16:11 NLT

*Joy is not necessarily the absence of suffering, it is the presence of God.*
SAM STORMS

Rejoice in the Lord always: and again I say, Rejoice.
PHILIPPIANS 4:4 KJV

When anxiety was great within me,
your consolation brought me joy.
PSALM 94:19 TNIV

Count it all joy, my brothers, when you meet trials of various
kinds, for you know that the testing of your faith produces
steadfastness.
JAMES 1:2–3 ESV

> *Be merry, really merry. The life of a true Christian should be a*
> *perpetual jubilee, a prelude to the festivals of eternity.*
> THEOPHANE VENARD

The Lord gives me strength. He is like a shield that keeps me
safe. My heart trusts in him, and he helps me. My heart jumps
for joy. I will sing and give thanks to him.
PSALM 28:7 NIrV

The hope of the righteous brings joy, but the expectation
of the wicked will perish.
PROVERBS 10:28 ESV

If you keep my commands, you will remain in my love, just as I have
kept my Father's commands and remain in his love. I have told you
this so that my joy may be in you and that your joy may be complete.
JOHN 15:10–11 NIV

> *As Christians, we shouldn't expect our joy to always feel like*
> *happiness, but instead recognize joy as inner security—*
> *a safeness in our life with Christ.*
> JILL BRISCOE

And an angel of the Lord appeared to them, and the glory of the Lord shone around them, and they were filled with fear. And the angel said to them, "Fear not, for behold, I bring you good news of great joy that will be for all the people. For unto you is born this day in the city of David a Savior, who is Christ the Lord."
LUKE 2:9–11 ESV

*The out-and-out Christian is a joyful Christian.*
ALEXANDER MACLAREN

Worship the LORD with gladness. Come before him, singing with joy.
PSALM 100:2 NLT

But the fruit of the Spirit is love, joy, peace, longsuffering, kindness, goodness, faithfulness.
GALATIANS 5:22 NKJV

Satisfy us in the morning with your unfailing love, that we may sing for joy and be glad all our days.
PSALM 90:14 NIV

# 38

## Knowledge

Knowledge is a good thing, and a higher education is usually a ticket to a profession with better wages—so it's worth the years of study. The Bible gives examples of men who applied themselves diligently to learning.

In many lines of work, you have to be a constant learner, frequently updating your information. Getting an education is not a one-time thing.

Of course, not all knowledge is profitable. Many people memorize reams of trivial knowledge, facts, and figures that are only good for impressing others, winning arguments, or for shouting out on a TV game show.

Having a lot of "head knowledge" tends to puff us up with pride.

Even as Christians, we can mistake Bible knowledge for wisdom, and come to think that knowing all about the Bible is a substitute for living its simple truths.

Knowledge is helpful, but wisdom—how to use knowledge for good—is even better. Being educated is an excellent thing but having integrity and love is better.

Moses was taught all the knowledge of the people of Egypt. He became a powerful speaker and a man of action.
ACTS 7:22 NIrV

As for these four young men, God gave them knowledge and skill in all literature and wisdom; and Daniel had understanding in all visions and dreams.
DANIEL 1:17 NKJV

Meanwhile a Jew named Apollos, a native of Alexandria, came to Ephesus. He was a learned man, with a thorough knowledge of the Scriptures.
ACTS 18:24 TNIV

*Books are wonderful mentors; they are available at any hour of the day or night. . . . No doubt God has spoken to me through books more than through any other source.*
BETTY SOUTHARD

If you have good sense, instruction will help you to have even better sense. And if you live right, education will help you to know even more.
PROVERBS 9:9 CEV

All the Athenians and the foreigners who lived there spent their time doing nothing but talking about and listening to the latest ideas.
ACTS 17:21 NIV

And further, by these, my son, be admonished: of making many books there is no end; and much study is a weariness of the flesh.
ECCLESIASTES 12:12 KJV

Remember, dear brothers and sisters, that few of you were wise in the world's eyes or powerful or wealthy when God called you. Instead, God chose things the world considers foolish in order to shame those who think they are wise.
1 CORINTHIANS 1:26–27 NLT

We know that "we all have knowledge." Knowledge inflates with pride, but love builds up. If anyone thinks he knows anything, he does not yet know it as he ought to know it.
1 CORINTHIANS 8:1–2 HCSB

They are always learning. But they never come to know the truth.
2 TIMOTHY 3:7 NIrV

*If in our pursuit of higher knowledge,*
*God seems to get smaller, we are being deceived.*
BETH MOORE

The fear of the LORD is the beginning of wisdom:
and the knowledge of the holy is understanding.
PROVERBS 9:10 KJV

They couldn't take their eyes off them—Peter and John standing there so confident, so sure of themselves! Their fascination deepened when they realized these two were laymen with no training in Scripture or formal education.
ACTS 4:13 MSG

Wisdom will protect you just like money; knowledge with good sense will lead you to life.
ECCLESIASTES 7:12 CEV

Wisdom is the most important thing; so get wisdom. If it costs everything you have, get understanding.
PROVERBS 4:7 NCV

*Be a learner and a listener. Spend more time gaining*
*wisdom and knowledge than giving it.*
STAN TOLER

# 39

## Leadership

Many of us don't like the word *leadership*. We may have worked under a few too many domineering bosses and inept overseers.

We also distrust political leaders because we feel they're self-serving and out of touch with the people they're supposed to be helping.

We're even leery of spiritual leadership, perhaps because we suspect that the pastor or the elders want to micromanage our lives.

But let's face it: part of the reason we're wary of leaders is that we don't want anyone telling us what to do. We value our independence and individualism too much.

Nevertheless, workplaces, cities, nations—even churches—require leadership.

Jesus gave the solution: leaders should be servants. If we're in a leadership position, we should use our authority wisely and govern others in a spirit of humility. We should genuinely care for our subordinates.

And if we take orders from some boss, or if God has given us spiritual overseers, we should ditch our pride and accept their instruction.

May the LORD. . .appoint a man over the congregation, who will go out and come in before them, and who will lead them out and bring them in, so that the congregation of the LORD will not be like sheep which have no shepherd.
NUMBERS 27:16–17 NASB

No one is as intelligent or wise as you are. You will be in charge of my court, and all my people will take orders from you.
GENESIS 41:39–40 NLT

*The higher the leadership the deeper the servanthood.*
STEVE CAMPBELL

Jesus said to them, "The kings of the nations hold power over
their people. And those who order them around call themselves
Protectors. But you must not be like that. Instead, the most
important among you should be like the youngest. The one who
rules should be like the one who serves."
LUKE 22:25–26 NIrV

You've observed how godless rulers throw their weight around,"
he said, "and when people get a little power how quickly it goes
to their heads. It's not going to be that way with you. Whoever
wants to be great must become a servant.
MARK 10:42–43 MSG

*If you go after the money and don't care about the people, we're
hirelings and not shepherds.*
A. W. TOZER

And I will give you shepherds after my own heart, who will feed
you with knowledge and understanding.
JEREMIAH 3:15 ESV

Woe to you shepherds of Israel who only take care of yourselves!
Should not shepherds take care of the flock? . . . You have
not strengthened the weak or healed the sick or bound up the
injured. You have not brought back the strays or searched for the
lost. You have ruled them harshly and brutally.
EZEKIEL 34:2, 4 NIV

Care for the flock that God has entrusted to you. Watch over it willingly, not grudgingly—not for what you will get out of it, but because you are eager to serve God. Don't lord it over the people assigned to your care, but lead them by your own good example.
1 PETER 5:2–3 NLT

*Leadership is about influencing people for good. It is about accomplishing more through others than we could ever do on our own.*
HANS FINZEL

Again Jesus said, "Simon son of John, do you love me?" He answered, "Yes, Lord, you know that I love you." Jesus said, "Take care of my sheep."
JOHN 21:16 NIV

Remember your leaders who taught you the word of God. Think of all the good that has come from their lives, and follow the example of their faith.
HEBREWS 13:7 NLT

Be responsive to your pastoral leaders. Listen to their counsel. They are alert to the condition of your lives and work under the strict supervision of God.
HEBREWS 13:17 MSG

*No man is worthy to rule until he has been ruled; no man can lead well until he has given himself to leadership greater than his own.*
CATHERINE MARSHALL

# 40

## Legacy

A legacy is what a man leaves behind for his children when his life is over. Often this means an inheritance of tangible, physical possessions. It may include a memorial.

A legacy is also what a man is remembered for; it is the sum total of his life, the enduring impact that he has on his children and succeeding generations.

As Christians, it is our responsibility to leave a godly legacy behind. We should want our children to remember that we lived for the truth, and our words and example should inspire them to be faithful to Christ as well, after we are gone.

Think of the enduring legacy that great men of God like Martin Luther or David Livingstone have left for the entire Church—and nations.

It's wonderful to leave a material inheritance for those we love, but it's far better to leave them a spiritual inheritance. We do this the same way we would build a financial legacy—by daily, consistently investing in it.

A good person leaves an inheritance for their children's children, but a sinner's wealth is stored up for the righteous.
PROVERBS 13:22 NIV

Home and wealth are inherited from fathers, but a sensible wife comes from the LORD.
PROVERBS 19:14 GW

A good name is to be more desired than great wealth, favor is better than silver and gold.
PROVERBS 22:1 NASB

*It's time to realize that it's not going to matter how much money you leave your family when you die. What is important is how much of yourself you leave with them.*

MARTHA BOLTON

I will teach you lessons from the past—things we have heard and known, things our ancestors have told us. We will not hide them from their descendants; we will tell the next generation the praiseworthy deeds of the LORD, his power, and the wonders he has done. He decreed statutes for Jacob and established the law in Israel, which he commanded our ancestors to teach their children, so the next generation would know them, even the children yet to be born, and they in turn would tell their children.

PSALM 78:2–6 TNIV

*Long after whatever personal investments you may leave your children are spent, a spiritual legacy will only compound daily and pay rich dividends throughout all eternity.*

PATRICK HENRY

So we Recabites have obeyed everything Jonadab our ancestor commanded us. Neither we nor our wives, sons, or daughters ever drink wine. We never build houses in which to live, or own fields or vineyards, or plant crops. We have lived in tents and have obeyed everything our ancestor Jonadab commanded us.

JEREMIAH 35:8–10 NCV

*The true legacy of a servant will not be determined by what he has done but by what others do as a result of what he has done.*

WAYNE CORDEIRO

They are the people of Israel. They have been adopted as God's children. God's glory belongs to them. So do the covenants. They received the law. They were taught to worship in the temple. They were given the promises. The founders of our nation belong to them. Christ comes from their family line.

ROMANS 9:4–5 NIrV

I'm reminded of how sincere your faith is. That faith first lived in your grandmother Lois and your mother Eunice. I'm convinced that it also lives in you.

2 TIMOTHY 1:5 GW

A good and honest life is a blessed memorial;
a wicked life leaves a rotten stench.

PROVERBS 10:7 MSG

Remember me, my God, for good, according to all that I have done for this people.

NEHEMIAH 5:19 NKJV

# 41

## Legalism

When we think of legalism, we usually think of the scribes and the Pharisees, men so obsessed with keeping every tiny dot of Moses' Law—and their own piled-on legal code—that they forgot about virtues such as love and mercy.

However, at times all of us have a tendency to be legalistic—and some of us have more of a struggle than others.

But rules are made to be obeyed, aren't they? Yes, they are. And most legalistic men are simply trying to obey God and live exemplary lives.

The danger comes, however, when we forget that we and others are justified (made righteous) by God's grace, and begin to think that rule-keeping is what gives us merit.

At that point we become self-righteous—and people around us notice it, usually because we've tried to impose our legal code on them. Or we've judged them for tiny infractions of our rules.

Keeping the rules is important, but let's not forget mercy and forgiveness.

Do not judge, or you too will be judged. For in the same way you judge others, you will be judged, and with the measure you use, it will be measured to you.
MATTHEW 7:1–2 TNIV

For judgment is without mercy to the one who has shown no mercy. Mercy triumphs over judgment.
JAMES 2:13 NKJV

*We want justice for others, mercy for ourselves.*
DAVID B. HAWKINS

He has not treated us as we deserve for our sins or paid us back for our wrongs. As high as the heavens are above the earth—that is how vast his mercy is toward those who fear him.
PSALM 103:10–11 GW

So why are you now trying to out-god God, loading these new believers down with rules that crushed our ancestors and crushed us, too?
ACTS 15:10 MSG

> *At its heart, legalism is a desire to appear holy. It is trying to be justified before men and not God.*
> DAVID WILKERSON

For, being ignorant of the righteousness of God, and seeking to establish their own, they did not submit to God's righteousness.
ROMANS 10:3 ESV

The written Law kills, but the Spirit gives life.
2 CORINTHIANS 3:6 NIrV

You pay a tenth of mint, dill, and cumin, yet you have neglected the more important matters of the law—justice, mercy, and faith. . . . You strain out a gnat, yet gulp down a camel!
MATTHEW 23:23–24 HCSB

> *Legalism forms when the rules get ahead of the relationship and begin to govern a person's life more than God's Spirit does.*
> JEFFREY MILLER

He that is without sin among you, let him first cast a stone at her.
JOHN 8:7 KJV

*Judgmentalism. . .is that ugly refusal to acknowledge that*
*"there but for the grace of God go I."*
PAUL COPAN

Do nothing from rivalry or conceit, but in humility count others
more significant than yourselves.
PHILIPPIANS 2:3 ESV

Jesus told a story to some people who thought they were better
than others and who looked down on everyone else.
LUKE 18:9 CEV

Why do you look at the speck that is in your brother's eye, but
do not notice the log that is in your own eye? Or how can you
say to your brother, 'Brother, let me take out the speck that is in
your eye,' when you yourself do not see the log that is in your
own eye? You hypocrite, first take the log out of your own eye,
and then you will see clearly to take out the speck that is in your
brother's eye.
LUKE 6:41–42 NASB

# 42

## Loving Others

The Bible tells us that "God is love." Love motivates Him in everything He does. That's why He wants love to be the basis of our actions as well.

God's two greatest commands are to love: we are to love Him with all our hearts, and we are to love our neighbors as ourselves. God loves people and He asks us to as well.

In fact, we literally prove our love for God by our love for our fellow man. The Bible bluntly tells us that we can't say that we love God if we hate our fellow man.

We are even to love our enemies, and by extension that includes family members who've offended us and coworkers who aggravate us. And we are not simply to think that we love them or say that we love them—we are to prove it by our actions.

It's a tall order, but God will give us that love if we ask Him for it.

My dear, dear friends, if God loved us like this, we certainly ought to love each other. No one has seen God, ever. But if we love one another, God dwells deeply within us, and his love becomes complete in us —perfect love!
1 JOHN 4:11–12 MSG

A new command I give you: Love one another. As I have loved you, so you must love one another. By this everyone will know that you are my disciples, if you love one another.
JOHN 13:34–35 NIV

> *There is no mystery about it. We love others, we love everybody,*
> *we love our enemies, because He first loved us.*
> HENRY DRUMMOND

But here is what I tell you. Love your enemies.
Pray for those who hurt you.
MATTHEW 5:44 NIrV

And this is his command: to believe in the name of his Son,
Jesus Christ, and to love one another as he commanded us.
1 JOHN 3:23 NIV

Love each other with genuine affection, and take delight
in honoring each other.
ROMANS 12:10 NLT

*I want the love that cannot help but love;*
*loving, like God, for the very sake of love.*
A. B. SIMPSON

Be completely humble and gentle; be patient, bearing with one
another in love. Make every effort to keep the unity of the Spirit
through the bond of peace.
EPHESIANS 4:2–3 NIV

Owe no one anything, except to love each other, for the one who
loves another has fulfilled the law. For the commandments, "You
shall not commit adultery, You shall not murder, You shall not steal,
You shall not covet," and any other commandment, are summed up
in this word: "You shall love your neighbor as yourself."
ROMANS 13:8–9 ESV

*Love is an act of endless forgiveness.*
JEAN VANIER

Beloved, let us love one another, for love is from God; and everyone who loves is born of God and knows God. The one who does not love does not know God, for God is love.
1 JOHN 4:7–8 NASB

But if anyone has the world's goods and sees his brother in need, yet closes his heart against him, how does God's love abide in him?
1 JOHN 3:17 ESV

My children, we should love people not only with words and talk, but by our actions and true caring.
1 JOHN 3:18 NCV

# 43

*Lust*

Lust is not the act of sexual sin—it's the desire that leads up to it and drives it. Therefore the Bible makes it clear that we must nip sinful thoughts in the bud.

The tenth commandment states, "You shall not covet your neighbor's wife"—which means, "You shall not lust after her." And Jesus said not to even look at a woman lustfully.

However, although we know that the Bible speaks clearly against sexual sin—so we avoid that—when it comes to our thoughts, we often question whether it's possible to refrain from lust.

Yes, it is. And we must, because of the damage that lust causes.

We can't not see a beautiful woman, but we can keep our eyes from lingering. It might not be possible to avoid a passing desire, but if we've made up our mind not to entertain such desires, they do pass.

It's not easy at first. It takes persistence until avoiding lustful thoughts becomes habit. Self-control is a fruit of the Spirit, but we must cultivate it.

And it came to pass after these things that his master's wife cast longing eyes on Joseph, and she said, "Lie with me." But he refused and said. . . . "How then can I do this great wickedness, and sin against God?" So it was, as she spoke to Joseph day by day, that he did not heed her, to lie with her or to be with her.
GENESIS 39:7–10 NKJV

No lusting after your neighbor's house—or wife or servant or maid. . . . Don't set your heart on anything that is your neighbor's.
EXODUS 20:17 MSG

*Lust is in opposition to love. It means to set your heart
and passions on something forbidden.*
STEPHEN AND ALEX KENDRICK

You have heard that it was said to those of old, "You shall not
commit adultery." But I say to you that whoever looks at a woman
to lust for her has already committed adultery with her
in his heart.
MATTHEW 5:27–28 NKJV

"That which proceeds out of the man, that is what defiles the
man. For from within, out of the heart of men, proceed the evil
thoughts, fornications, thefts, murders, adulteries."
MARK 7:20–21 NASB

I promised myself never to stare with desire at a young woman.
JOB 31:1 CEV

*Lust is the Devil's counterfeit for love. There is nothing more beautiful
on earth than a pure love and there is nothing so blighting as lust.*
D. L. MOODY

They commit adultery with their eyes, and their desire
for sin is never satisfied.
2 PETER 2:14 NLT

Flee fornication. Every sin that a man doeth is without the body;
but he that committeth fornication sinneth against his own body.
1 CORINTHIANS 6:18 KJV

God's will is for you to be holy, so stay away from all sexual sin.
1 THESSALONIANS 4:3 NLT

*Are you toying with sin? If so, for yourself, your family, and your Lord—stop. Don't put yourself in a position of compromise.*

CHUCK COLSON

So do you think we should continue sinning so that God will give us even more grace? No! We died to our old sinful lives, so how can we continue living with sin?

ROMANS 6:1–2 NCV

But sexual immorality and all impurity or covetousness must not even be named among you, as is proper among saints.

EPHESIANS 5:3 ESV

# 44

## Mentoring

A mentor, by definition, is a wise and trusted teacher, usually an older, more experienced man. Mentoring is the relationship between the mentor and a less experienced man.

It's not the same thing as coaching, since the mentor has no power to make anyone do what he says. He's just there to share from his experience, give advice, pass on knowledge, and come alongside the younger man like a guidance counselor.

Mentoring is often used in business or political circles, but has proved to be very useful in the Church as well, since discipling (instructing and training) others is a vital part of the Christian faith.

Mentoring is particularly beneficial when a man makes himself accountable to his mentor, and is honest and open about his struggles.

The mentor must teach as much by example as by word. A good mentor will not try to make another man into his disciple, but will lead him to become a better disciple of Jesus, the master Shepherd.

*The value of mentoring derives from the value of relationships.*
HOWARD AND WILLIAM HENDRICKS

Follow my example, as I follow the example of Christ.
1 CORINTHIANS 11:1 NIV

Brothers and sisters, all of you should try to follow my example and to copy those who live the way we showed you.
PHILIPPIANS 3:17 NCV

Follow what you heard from me as the pattern of true teaching.
Follow it with faith and love because you belong to Christ Jesus.
2 Timothy 1:13 NIrV

> *Show me a man's closest companions and I can make a*
> *fairly accurate guess as to what sort of man he is, as well as what*
> *sort of man he is likely to become.*
> Howard and William Hendricks

And the things that you have heard from me among many witnesses,
commit these to faithful men who will be able to teach others also.
2 Timothy 2:2 NKJV

Preach the word; be prepared in season and out of season;
correct, rebuke and encourage—with great patience
and careful instruction.
2 Timothy 4:2 NIV

Philip ran up and heard him reading Isaiah the prophet, and said,
"Do you understand what you are reading?" And he said, "Well,
how could I, unless someone guides me?" And he invited Philip
to come up and sit with him.
Acts 8:30–31 NASB

Think how you have instructed many, how you have strengthened
feeble hands. Your words have supported those who stumbled;
you have strengthened faltering knees.
Job 4:3–4 TNIV

If you correct the wise, they will be all the wiser.
Proverbs 19:25 NLT

*Your best friends will criticize you privately and encourage you publicly.*
BRUCE BICKEL AND STAN JANTZ

Correction and self-control will lead you through life.
PROVERBS 6:23 CEV

The ear that listens to life-giving reproof will dwell among the
wise. Whoever ignores instruction despises himself, but he who
listens to reproof gains intelligence.
PROVERBS 15:31–32 ESV

You use steel to sharpen steel, and one friend sharpens another.
PROVERBS 27:17 MSG

*Accountability will not work unless there is real honesty and
vulnerability between the men regarding their struggles and shortfalls.*
TOM EISENMAN

Confess your faults one to another, and pray one for another,
that ye may be healed.
JAMES 5:16 KJV

Perfume and incense bring joy to the heart, and the pleasantness
of a friend springs from their heartfelt advice.
PROVERBS 27:9 NIV

# 45

## Patience

According to the dictionary, patience is "the calm endurance of hardship, provocation, pain, delay, etc." The etc. includes shortcomings, failures, and aggravating habits.

Fortunately for us, God is very patient with His people. Stated quite plainly, He puts up with a lot from us. He does this because of His great love.

He is also patient with us because, even though we don't grow spiritually as fast or as much as we should—or we are slow to obey—He doesn't give up hope in us. His Holy Spirit keeps working in our lives, helping us see what He's trying to teach us.

God also instructs us to be patient with our fellow human beings—to be kind and to bear with others in love. Impatience, demanding immediate results or insisting on perfect behavior, only frustrates us and discourages others.

Finally, God tells us to be patient with Him, to trust Him and to wait patiently when He delays answering our prayers.

Then he passed in front of Moses and called out, "I am the LORD God. I am merciful and very patient with my people. I show great love, and I can be trusted."
EXODUS 34:6 CEV

The LORD is merciful! He is kind and patient,
and his love never fails.
PSALM 103:8 CEV

Be still before the LORD and wait patiently for him;
do not fret when people succeed in their ways,
when they carry out their wicked schemes.
PSALM 37:7 NIV

*Patience with others is Love, patience with self is Hope,*
*patience with God is Faith.*
ADEL BESTAVROS

Wait patiently for the LORD. Be brave and courageous.
Yes, wait patiently for the LORD.
PSALM 27:14 NLT

And the Scriptures give us hope and encouragement as we wait
patiently for God's promises to be fulfilled.
ROMANS 15:4 NLT

*Teach us, O Lord, the disciplines of patience,*
*for to wait is often harder than to work.*
PETER MARSHALL

Better to be patient than powerful; better to have self-control
than to conquer a city.
PROVERBS 16:32 NLT

When you hope, be joyful. When you suffer, be patient.
When you pray, be faithful.
ROMANS 12:12 NIrV

Love is patient, love is kind and is not jealous; love does not brag
and is not arrogant.
1 CORINTHIANS 13:4 NASB

Therefore, as God's chosen people, holy and dearly loved, clothe
yourselves with compassion, kindness, humility,
gentleness and patience.
COLOSSIANS 3:12 NIV

Be completely humble and gentle; be patient, bearing with one another in love.
EPHESIANS 4:2 NIV

*Biblically, waiting is not just something we have to do until we get what we want. Waiting is part of the process of becoming what God wants us to be.*
JOHN ORTBERG

I pray that the Lord will guide you to be as loving as God and as patient as Christ.
2 THESSALONIANS 3:5 CEV

The Lord's bond-servant must not be quarrelsome, but be kind to all, able to teach, patient when wronged.
2 TIMOTHY 2:24 NASB

*The principle part of faith is patience.*
GEORGE MACDONALD

For God is pleased with you when you do what you know is right and patiently endure unfair treatment. Of course, you get no credit for being patient if you are beaten for doing wrong. But if you suffer for doing good and endure it patiently, God is pleased with you.
1 PETER 2:19–20 NLT

*Endeavor to be always patient of the faults and imperfections of others, for thou hast many faults and imperfections of thy own that require a reciprocation of forbearance.*
THOMAS À KEMPIS

# 46

## Peace

Jesus is the Prince of Peace, and by dying on the cross He brought us peace with God. For those of us who experienced neglect or abuse, a sinful lifestyle, addictions, and broken relationships, that peace was especially sweet when we first experienced it.

We're not supposed to just have peace when we're first saved, however—then watch it fade to be replaced by a troubled mind again.

God's desire is that Christ's peace stays with us and rules in our hearts daily. That, of course, is our desire as well. But how do we keep it? We keep it by spending time every day praying, reading God's Word, and praising Him.

We will have perfect peace when we love and trust God, because then we won't worry about calamities or feel condemned over our stumblings.

When our hearts are filled with peace, we can live in peace with others. We're also able to bring peace into troubled relationships and situations around us.

For to us a child is born, to us a son is given, and the government will be on his shoulders. And he will be called Wonderful Counselor, Mighty God, Everlasting Father, Prince of Peace.
ISAIAH 9:6 NIV

Therefore, since we have been justified by faith, we have peace with God through our Lord Jesus Christ.
ROMANS 5:1 ESV

For the mind set on the flesh is death, but the mind set on the Spirit is life and peace,
ROMANS 8:6 NASB

*Peace with God does not always mean a calm time of happiness.*
*The salvation that Jesus brought comes with a price:*
*conflict against evil. But in the end, all who trust in*
*Him experience the peace of eternal life.*

The LORD bless you, and keep you; the LORD make His face shine
on you, and be gracious to you; the LORD lift up His countenance
on you, and give you peace.
NUMBERS 6:24–26 NASB

The LORD gives strength to his people;
the LORD blesses his people with peace.
PSALM 29:11 NIV

Those who love Your law have great peace,
and nothing causes them to stumble.
PSALM 119:165 NASB

And let the peace that comes from Christ rule in your hearts.
For as members of one body you are called to live in peace.
And always be thankful.
COLOSSIANS 3:15 NLT

*God cannot give us happiness and peace apart from Himself,*
*because it is not there. There is no such thing.*
C. S. LEWIS

Peace I leave with you, My peace I give to you; not as the world
gives do I give to you. Let not your heart be troubled,
neither let it be afraid.
JOHN 14:27 NKJV

In peace I will lie down and sleep, for you alone, O Lord,
will keep me safe.
PSALM 4:8 NLT

> *Peacemakers carry about with them an atmosphere*
> *in which quarrels die a natural death.*
> R. T. ARCHIBALD

Blessed are the peacemakers:
for they shall be called the children of God.
MATTHEW 5:9 KJV

If it is possible, as far as it depends on you,
live at peace with everyone.
ROMANS 12:18 NIV

Finally, brothers, rejoice. Aim for restoration, comfort one another,
agree with one another, live in peace; and the God of love and
peace will be with you.
2 CORINTHIANS 13:11 ESV

> *And therefore you who think so basely of the Gospel and the professors*
> *of it, because at present their peace and comfort are not come, should*
> *know that it is on the way to them, and comes to stay everlastingly*
> *with them. . . . Look not how the Christian begins, but ends.*
> WILLIAM GURNALL

The Lord gives perfect peace to those whose faith is firm.
ISAIAH 26:3 CEV

# 47

## Perseverance

Perseverance means being persistent. It means not giving up when the road gets rough or dark or monotonous, but being determined to reach the goal because we trust that we'll be richly rewarded for our efforts.

The Bible clearly says that following Jesus often means to invite hardship into our life. We're called to deny ourselves and to resist temptation that would pull us off the path.

Jesus praised Christians who persevered and endured hardships for His name, and who had not grown weary, lost heart, and thrown in the towel.

He also pointed out the need to persevere in prayer. Too often Christians give up when the answer doesn't materialize immediately. We frequently must keep believing and praying when our way gets dark, and that requires sustained effort.

In the Greek, the familiar phrase, "Ask and it shall be given you" literally means, "Ask and keep on asking and it shall be given you."

So keep on. Don't give up.

You need to persevere so that when you have done the will of God, you will receive what he has promised.
HEBREWS 10:36 TNIV

We say they are happy because they did not give up. You have heard about Job's patience, and you know the Lord's purpose for him in the end.
JAMES 5:11 NCV

*The secret of endurance is to remember that your pain is temporary but your reward will be eternal.*
RICK WARREN

*Determination is the refusal to accept defeat as final.*
STEVE CAMPBELL

Then Jacob was left alone, and a man wrestled with him until daybreak. . . . Then he said, "Let me go, for the dawn is breaking." But he said, "I will not let you go unless you bless me."
GENESIS 32:24, 26 NASB

Then He spoke a parable to them, that men always ought to pray and not lose heart, saying: "There was in a certain city a judge who did not fear God nor regard man. Now there was a widow in that city; and she came to him, saying, 'Get justice for me from my adversary.' And he would not for a while; but afterward he said within himself, 'Though I do not fear God nor regard man, yet because this widow troubles me I will avenge her, lest by her continual coming she weary me.' " Then the Lord said, "Hear what the unjust judge said. And shall God not avenge His own elect who cry out day and night to Him, though He bears long with them?"
LUKE 18:1–7 NKJV

*Refuse to settle for anything less than everything God has for you.*
JOYCE MEYER

And when he heard that it was Jesus of Nazareth, he began to cry out and say, "Jesus, Son of David, have mercy on me!" And many rebuked him, telling him to be silent. But he cried out all the more, "Son of David, have mercy on me!"
MARK 10:47–48 ESV

# 48

## Possessions

God is aware that we have physical needs—we require food, clothing, and shelter—and He has instructed us to work to earn them.

He also promises to bless us so that we have abundance.

God knows, however, the affect that wealth often has on us: one of the first things we do when we prosper is to buy "nice things" for ourselves. We usually begin to fill our rooms with luxuries.

We set our heart on our possessions and experience grief if any of them are damaged or lost. While we believe in eternal rewards in a world to come, we sometimes live as though we were going to live down here permanently. How easily we become covetous.

The solution to materialism is to keep our eyes on our heavenly rewards.

We are also wise to share of our abundance with the needy. This may seem too idealistic, even impractical, but Jesus commands it—not only for their sake, but for our own good.

As for every man to whom God has given riches and wealth, and given him power to eat of it, to receive his heritage and rejoice in his labor—this is the gift of God.
ECCLESIASTES 5:19 NKJV

The blessing of the LORD makes one rich,
and He adds no sorrow with it.
PROVERBS 10:22 NKJV

Even if your riches grow, don't put your trust in them.
PSALM 62:10 NIRV

When good things increase, the ones who consume them multiply; what, then, is the profit to the owner, except to gaze at them with his eyes?
ECCLESIASTES 5:11 HCSB

*Seek not great things for yourselves in this world, for if your garments be too long, they will make you stumble; and one staff helps a man in his journey, when many in his hands at once hinders him.*
WILLIAM BRIDGE

And he said to them, "Take care, and be on your guard against all covetousness, for one's life does not consist in the abundance of his possessions."
LUKE 12:15 ESV

Sell your possessions and give to those in need. This will store up treasure for you in heaven! And the purses of heaven never get old or develop holes. Your treasure will be safe; no thief can steal it and no moth can destroy it.
LUKE 12:33 NLT

*There are three conversions necessary: the conversion of the heart, mind, and the purse.*
MARTIN LUTHER

Jesus answered, "If you want to be perfect, go, sell your possessions and give to the poor, and you will have treasure in heaven. Then come, follow me." When the young man heard this, he went away sad, because he had great wealth.
MATTHEW 19:21–22 NIV

Zaccheus stopped and said to the Lord, "Behold, Lord, half of my possessions I will give to the poor, and if I have defrauded anyone of anything, I will give back four times as much." And Jesus said to him, "Today salvation has come to this house, because he, too, is a son of Abraham."
LUKE 19:8–9 NASB

*To dispense our wealth liberally, is the best way to preserve it.*
ISAAC BARROW

But if anyone has the world's goods and sees his brother in need, yet closes his heart against him, how does God's love abide in him?
1 JOHN 3:17 ESV

Now the multitude of those who believed were of one heart and one soul; neither did anyone say that any of the things he possessed was his own, but they had all things in common.
ACTS 4:32 NKJV

You suffered along with those who were thrown into jail, and when all you owned was taken from you, you accepted it with joy. You knew there were better things waiting for you that will last forever.
HEBREWS 10:34 NLT

If I give all I possess to the poor and give over my body to hardship that I may boast, but do not have love, I gain nothing.
1 CORINTHIANS 13:3 NIV

We didn't bring anything into the world, and we can't take anything out of it. As long as we have food and clothes, we should be satisfied.
1 TIMOTHY 6:7–8 GW

# 49

*Power*

God is not only powerful, He is all-powerful. (That's what omnipotent means.) He has the strength and the might to do absolutely anything. He created the entire world and the universe, after all, so nothing is too hard for Him.

Unfortunately, we often strive to accomplish things in our own power and ability as though everything depended upon us.

Yet the Bible urges us to look to the Lord for strength and expect Him to do miracles.

Certainly we are to do what we can do, but we will often find ourselves in situations where we either have no power to do what needs to be done—or not enough.

Jesus was filled with the power of the Holy Spirit and performed astonishing miracles. The Bible urges us to let the Spirit take control of our lives as well. This is especially vital if we are to do God's work and win souls to Christ.

Ask God to show His power in your life today!

Your right hand, O LORD, is majestic in power, Your right hand, O LORD, shatters the enemy.
EXODUS 15:6 NASB

Yours, LORD, is the greatness and the power and the glory and the majesty and the splendor, for everything in heaven and earth is yours.
1 CHRONICLES 29:11 NIV

> *God's power is like Himself: infinite, eternal, incomprehensible; it can neither be checked, restrained, nor frustrated by the creature.*
> STEPHEN CHARNOCK

The Good News is about his Son. In his earthly life he was born into King David's family line, and he was shown to be the Son of God when he was raised from the dead by the power of the Holy Spirit. He is Jesus Christ our Lord.
ROMANS 1:3–4 NLT

And all the people were trying to touch Him, for power was coming from Him and healing them all.
LUKE 6:19 NASB

> *If we think of the Holy Spirit only as an impersonal power or influence, then our thought will constantly be, how can I get hold of and use the Holy Spirit; but if we think of Him in the biblical way as a divine Person. . .then our thought will constantly be, "How can the Holy Spirit get hold of and use me?"*
> R. A. TORREY

Look to the LORD and his strength; seek his face always.
PSALM 105:4 TNIV

But you will receive power when the Holy Spirit comes upon you. And you will be my witnesses, telling people about me everywhere—in Jerusalem, throughout Judea, in Samaria, and to the ends of the earth.
ACTS 1:8 NLT

And with great power the apostles were giving their testimony to the resurrection of the Lord Jesus, and great grace was upon them all.
ACTS 4:33 ESV

God's kingdom isn't just a lot of words. It is power.
1 CORINTHIANS 4:20 CEV

I pray that God, the source of hope, will fill you completely with joy and peace because you trust in him. Then you will overflow with confident hope through the power of the Holy Spirit.
ROMANS 15:13 NLT

*If you are strangers to prayer you are strangers to power.*
BILLY SUNDAY

You won't succeed by might or by power, but by my Spirit, says the LORD of Armies.
ZECHARIAH 4:6 GW

Finally, my brethren, be strong in the Lord, and in the power of his might.
EPHESIANS 6:10 KJV

He giveth power to the faint; and to them that have no might he increaseth strength.
ISAIAH 40:29 KJV

*If you look up into His face and say, "Yes, Lord, whatever it costs," at that moment He'll flood your life with His presence and power.*
ALAN REDPATH

I am not ashamed of the gospel, because it is the power of God that brings salvation to everyone who believes.
ROMANS 1:16 NIV

For the word of the cross is folly to those who are perishing, but to us who are being saved it is the power of God.
1 CORINTHIANS 1:18 ESV

# 50

## Prayer

We enjoy communicating with someone we love, or with a friend whose company we enjoy. If we have a confidant who truly cares about us and understands us—and has the power to help us—we don't hesitate to call him.

God is all of these things and more. We have a relationship with Jesus that goes deeper than any human friendship.

We can turn to God in our time of desperate need, and He hears us. He may not answer in the exact way or time frame we desire, but if we ask in faith, He will answer. Mind you, we have to persevere in prayer at times.

We shouldn't just pray when we face an emergency, however. We should talk to God constantly. We should come into His presence by worshiping Him, present our petitions, then wait, trusting Him to answer.

Instead of wasting our time worrying about problems, we should pray about them. God has the power to change our circumstances.

Pray in the Spirit at all times and on every occasion. Stay alert and be persistent in your prayers for all believers everywhere.
EPHESIANS 6:18 NLT

Pray without ceasing.
1 THESSALONIANS 5:17 KJV

Rejoice in hope, be patient in tribulation, be constant in prayer.
ROMANS 12:12 ESV

Do not be anxious about anything, but in every situation, by prayer and petition, with thanksgiving, present your requests to God.
PHILIPPIANS 4:6 NIV

*Never wait for fitter time or place to talk to Him. To wait till you go to church or to your closet is to make Him wait. He will listen as you walk.*
GEORGE MACDONALD

Are any of you in trouble? Then you should pray.
JAMES 5:13 NIrV

Answer me when I call to you, my righteous God. Give me relief from my distress; have mercy on me and hear my prayer.
PSALM 4:1 NIV

He will respond to the prayer of the destitute;
he will not despise their plea.
PSALM 102:17 NIV

*We are too busy to pray, and so we are too busy to have power. We have a great deal of activity, but we accomplish little; many services but few conversions; much machinery but few results.*
R. A. TORREY

The LORD has heard my plea; the LORD accepts my prayer.
PSALM 6:9 ESV

But when you pray, go into your room, close the door and pray to your Father, who is unseen. Then your Father, who sees what is done in secret, will reward you. And when you pray, do not keep on babbling like pagans, for they think they will be heard because of their many words. Do not be like them, for your Father knows what you need before you ask him.
MATTHEW 6:6–8 NIV

And all things you ask in prayer, believing, you will receive.
MATTHEW 21:22 NASB

The prayer of a godly person is powerful. It makes things happen.
JAMES 5:16 NIrV

*Invariable "success" in prayer would not prove the Christian doctrine
at all. It would prove something more like magic—a power in certain
human beings to control, or compel, the course of nature.*
C. S. LEWIS

This, then, is how you should pray: "Our Father in heaven,
hallowed be your name, your kingdom come, your will be done,
on earth as it is in heaven. Give us today our daily bread. And
forgive us our debts, as we also have forgiven our debtors. And
lead us not into temptation, but deliver us from the evil one."
MATTHEW 6:9–13 NIV

*On days when life is difficult and I feel overwhelmed, as I do fairly
often, it helps to remember in my prayers that all God requires of me is
to trust Him and be His friend. I find I can do that.*
BRUCE LARSON

# 51

*Pride*

The Bible speaks strongly against pride, calling it a sin and an evil.

When it warns against pride, however, it's not talking about a healthy sense of self-esteem, nor a person's right to accept acclaim and feel satisfied with a job well done.

God uses other words to describe sinful pride, such as haughty, vain, vainglorious, boastful, cocky, and arrogant. Even worldly people admit that these are undesirable traits.

A man full of pride is offensive to others—and to God. He is so self-confident that he feels little need to pray. In his opinion, those who depend on God are weak. He is so pumped about his looks, intellect, power, position, and ability that he feels no need for God.

A proud man literally sets himself up for a fall.

We may not feel we're that proud, but if our sense of importance and self-confidence make us think we don't need to depend on God, or don't need to pray, we're already too proud.

Proud eyes and a proud heart are the lamp of sinful people.
But those things are evil.
PROVERBS 21:4 NIrV

Mockers are proud and haughty;
they act with boundless arrogance.
PROVERBS 21:24 NLT

Where there is strife, there is pride, but wisdom is found
in those who take advice.
PROVERBS 13:10 NIV

*If I had only one sermon to preach it would be a sermon against pride.*
G. K. CHESTERTON

Your herds and flocks increase their numbers. You also get more and more silver and gold. And everything you have multiplies. Then your hearts will become proud. And you will forget the Lord your God.
DEUTERONOMY 8:13–14 NIrV

When I fed you, you were full. When you were full, you became arrogant. That is why you forgot me.
HOSEA 13:6 GW

In his pride the wicked man does not seek him; in all his thoughts there is no room for God.
PSALM 10:4 NIV

God opposes the proud but shows favor to the humble and oppressed.
JAMES 4:6 TNIV

*There is something within the human spirit that wants to resist the thought of weakness. Many times this is nothing more than our human pride at work. Just as weakness carries a great potential for strength, pride carries an equally great potential for defeat.*
CHARLES STANLEY

Pride goes before destruction, and haughtiness before a fall.
PROVERBS 16:18 NLT

A man's pride will bring him low, but the humble in spirit will retain honor.
PROVERBS 29:23 NKJV

The eyes of the arrogant will be humbled and human pride brought low; the LORD alone will be exalted in that day.
ISAIAH 2:11 TNIV

*God created the world out of nothing; so as long as we are nothing, he can make something out of us.*
MARTIN LUTHER

Believers in humble circumstances ought to take pride in their high position. But the rich should take pride in their humiliation—since they will pass away like a wild flower.
JAMES 1:9–10 NIV

Do your own work well, and then you will have something to be proud of. But don't compare yourself with others.
GALATIANS 6:4 CEV

Too much pride can put you to shame. It's wiser to be humble.
PROVERBS 11:2 CEV

# 52

## Procrastination

Procrastinate comes from the Latin root word *cras*, which means "tomorrow." When we procrastinate, we're putting off a task until later in the day—or "tomorrow."

If we keep putting it off, we may forget it entirely, and tomorrow becomes never.

There are several reasons why we procrastinate: sometimes we do so out of laziness; sometimes it's because we know a job will be hard and we're having trouble getting our brain in gear to do it.

When it means interrupting our schedule to handle a detail for someone, we may be too preoccupied or—so we tell ourselves—too busy.

The reality may be that we aren't concerned enough. "They can wait," we say, even though their operations grind to a halt or they suffer unnecessary hardship as a result.

The Bible tells us not to delay or be slow to pay someone what we owe them. We are likewise to lose no time in delivering a needed service, or helping others in their hour of urgent need.

Withhold not good from them to whom it is due, when it is in the power of thine hand to do it.
PROVERBS 3:27 KJV

Suppose you have a friend, and you go to him at midnight and say, "Friend, lend me three loaves of bread; a friend of mine on a journey has come to me, and I have no food to offer him." And suppose the one inside answers, "Don't bother me. The door is already locked, and my children and I are in bed. I can't get up and give you anything."
LUKE 11:5–7 NIV

Don't say to your neighbor, "Go away! Come back later.
I'll give it tomorrow"—when it is there with you.
PROVERBS 3:28 HCSB

> *Thou seest a needy person, and thou turnest away thine eye;*
> *but it is the Prince of Darkness that casts this mist upon thee.*
> JOHN DONNE

Each day you shall give him his wages, and not let the sun
go down on it, for he is poor and has set his heart on it;
lest he cry out against you to the LORD, and it be sin to you.
DEUTERONOMY 24:15 NKJV

You shall not delay the offering from your harvest and your vintage.
EXODUS 22:29 NASB

Rebekah arrived, her jug on her shoulder. She went to the spring
and drew water and I said, "Please, can I have a drink?" She
didn't hesitate. She held out her jug and said, "Drink; and when
you're finished I'll also water your camels."
GENESIS 24:45–46 MSG

If you make a vow to the LORD your God, do not be slow to pay it,
for the LORD your God will certainly demand it of you and you will
be guilty of sin.
DEUTERONOMY 23:21 TNIV

> *Tomorrow—it is not written in the almanack of time.*
> *Tomorrow—it is in Satan's calendar, and nowhere else. . . .*
> *Yonder clock saith "today"; everything crieth "today."*
> CHARLES H. SPURGEON

If someone is lazy, the roof will begin to fall. If he doesn't fix it, the house will leak.

ECCLESIASTES 10:18 NCV

*I was taught that laziness was one of the worst evils, and that there was dignity and honor in labor.*

BILLY GRAHAM

Abigail acted quickly. She took two hundred loaves of bread, two skins of wine, five dressed sheep, five seahs of roasted grain, a hundred cakes of raisins and two hundred cakes of pressed figs, and loaded them on donkeys.

1 SAMUEL 25:18 NIV

Since Lydda was near Joppa, the disciples, having heard that Peter was there, sent two men to him, imploring him, "Do not delay in coming to us." So Peter arose and went with them.

ACTS 9:38–39 NASB

When we have the opportunity to help anyone, we should do it.

GALATIANS 6:10 NCV

# 53

## Protection

The world is filled with dangers and threats, and God requires us to take the necessary steps to protect ourselves and our families from as many of them as we can.

For example, we install antivirus programs to protect our computers from viruses. We lock our house doors to prevent break-ins and theft. These things are common sense.

We should do what we can do to protect our families and possessions.

Nevertheless, we simply cannot protect our homes and loved ones from all dangers large or small. That's why we need to pray for God to do what we can't do, to protect us from danger we can't see or anticipate.

Trusting God doesn't usually negate us doing our part, however. Often our efforts and prayers work together.

There will be circumstances, however, when we're utterly powerless to protect ourselves from danger—and that's when we must depend wholly upon God to protect us.

That is when we must pray and trust.

If the LORD does not protect a city, it is useless for the guard to stay alert.
PSALM 127:1 GW

They all plotted together to come and fight against Jerusalem and stir up trouble against it. But we prayed to our God and posted a guard day and night to meet this threat.
NEHEMIAH 4:8–9 NIV

*Lord, You ask us to stay alert and watch; we must do our part.*
*But we still utterly depend on You. Protect us, O God!*

Do not be afraid of them. Remember the Lord, great and awesome, and fight for your brethren, your sons, your daughters, your wives, and your houses.
NEHEMIAH 4:14 NKJV

If the owner of the house had known at what time of night the thief was coming, he would have kept watch and would not have let his house be broken into.
MATTHEW 24:43 TNIV

The horse is made ready for the day of battle, but the victory belongs to the LORD.
PROVERBS 21:31 ESV

But Moses told the people, "Don't be afraid. Just stand still and watch the LORD rescue you today. The Egyptians you see today will never be seen again. The LORD himself will fight for you. Just stay calm."
EXODUS 14:13–14 NLT

*Safety does not depend on our conception of the absence of danger. Safety is found in God's presence, in the centre of His perfect will.*
T. J. BACH

"Be strong and courageous! Don't be afraid or discouraged before the king of Assyria or before all the multitude with him, for there are more with us than with him. He has only human strength, but we have the LORD our God to help us and to fight our battles."
2 CHRONICLES 32:7–8 HCSB

He saved me from my powerful enemies, from those who hated me, because they were too strong for me.
PSALM 18:17 NCV

Though I walk in the midst of trouble, thou wilt revive me: thou shalt stretch forth thine hand against the wrath of mine enemies, and thy right hand shall save me.
PSALM 138:7 KJV

*God knows that life can throw us up against a wall with no options and that the pain can be intense. But He stands vigil over us like a pillar of cloud and fire.*
ANGELA THOMAS

For you have been my refuge, a strong tower against the enemy.
PSALM 61:3 ESV

All of you worship the LORD, so you must trust him to help and protect you.
PSALM 115:11 CEV

The LORD helps them and delivers them; he delivers them from the wicked and saves them, because they take refuge in him.
PSALM 37:40 NIV

For the angel of the LORD is a guard; he surrounds and defends all who fear him.
PSALM 34:7 NLT

# 54

## Providing

The primary responsibility to provide for the needs of a family rests upon men. Certainly our task is easier if ours is a two-income home, but we are to be gainfully employed and to work hard to ensure that our loved ones don't lack.

Yet we are told to pray for God to "give us our daily bread," because when it comes right down to it, He is our ultimate provider. We depend upon Him.

We aren't as acutely aware of this fact when we're a salaried employee, but we certainly are if we operate a business in a fluctuating economy, depend upon contract work, run a farm, or earn a commission on sales—or if we get laid off from our job.

Then we realize how much we depend on the Lord!

The good news is, God has promised to provide for us. He may require us to tighten our belts and do without certain luxuries we considered essentials, but He will provide.

Anyone who does not provide for their relatives, and especially for their own household, has denied the faith and is worse than an unbeliever.
1 TIMOTHY 5:8 NIV

If you are a thief, quit stealing. Instead, use your hands for good hard work, and then give generously to others in need.
EPHESIANS 4:28 NLT

> *At the heart of mature masculinity is a sense of benevolent responsibility to lead, provide for and protect women.*
> JOHN PIPER AND ELISABETH ELLIOT

Work with your hands, just as we told you to. Then unbelievers will have respect for your everyday life. And you won't have to depend on anyone.
1 THESSALONIANS 4:11–12 NIrV

Yes, you yourselves know that these hands have provided for my necessities, and for those who were with me. I have shown you in every way, by laboring like this, that you must support the weak.
ACTS 20:34–35 NKJV

And let our people learn to devote themselves to good works, so as to help cases of urgent need, and not be unfruitful.
TITUS 3:14 ESV

> *Obedience to God's commands not only protects us from harm;*
> *it also allows God to provide for us, sometimes in breathtaking ways.*
> JOSH MCDOWELL AND BOB HOSTETLER

My God will use his wonderful riches in Christ Jesus to give you everything you need.
PHILIPPIANS 4:19 NCV

Don't worry and ask yourselves, "Will we have anything to eat? Will we have anything to drink? Will we have any clothes to wear?" Only people who don't know God are always worrying about such things. Your Father in heaven knows that you need all of these.
MATTHEW 6:31–32 CEV

You open your hand and satisfy the needs of every living creature.
PSALM 145:16 NIrV

The young lions lack and suffer hunger; but those who seek the
LORD shall not lack any good thing.
PSALM 34:10 NKJV

*He that feeds his birds will not starve his babes.*
MATTHEW HENRY

Not that I speak in regard to need, for I have learned in whatever
state I am, to be content. . . . Everywhere and in all things I have
learned both to be full and to be hungry, both to abound and to
suffer need.
PHILIPPIANS 4:11–12 NKJV

But if we have food and clothing, with these we will be content.
1 TIMOTHY 6:8 ESV

# 55

## Rest and Relaxation

We get so busy sometimes that we have trouble slowing down long enough to rest. We question whether we actually need to.

That's why God simply made it a commandment: take a day off once a week.

Then we reason that relaxing is the ideal, but that we don't live in an ideal world. We have so much to do we can't take time to simply be quiet, to meditate on God, go to church, or enjoy a nature walk.

To which God repeats: Rest.

We need to rest or we'll never renew our spirit, and we'll eventually burn out.

Besides taking a day off or unwinding at the end of a day, God talks about our need to live in a state of rest, even in the middle of a day's activities. We do this by dwelling in His presence and trusting Him.

When we're weary and carrying heavy burdens, Jesus invites us to come to Him. If we do, He will give us rest.

And he said unto them, Come ye yourselves apart into a desert place, and rest a while: for there were many coming and going, and they had no leisure so much as to eat.
MARK 6:31 KJV

And Isaac went out to meditate in the field at the eventide.
GENESIS 24:63 KJV

Consider the lilies of the field, how they grow.
MATTHEW 6:28 NKJV

And he said, "My presence will go with you, and I will give you rest."
EXODUS 33:14 ESV

*Renewal and restoration are not luxuries; they are essentials.*
*Being alone and resting for awhile is not selfish; it is Christlike.*
CHARLES SWINDOLL

So we arrived in Jerusalem, where we rested three days.
EZRA 8:32 TNIV

Six days do your work, but on the seventh day do not work,
so that your ox and your donkey may rest, and so that the slave
born in your household and the foreigner living among you may
be refreshed.
EXODUS 23:12 NIV

God will speak to this people, to whom he said, "This is the
resting place, let the weary rest"; and, "This is the place of
repose"—but they would not listen.
ISAIAH 28:11–12 TNIV

*The restless, high-pressure hurry in which men live endangers the very*
*foundations of personal religion.*
JOHN CHARLES RYLE

For thus saith the Lord GOD, the Holy One of Israel; In returning
and rest shall ye be saved; in quietness and in confidence shall
be your strength: and ye would not.
ISAIAH 30:15 KJV

The LORD is my shepherd; I shall not want. He maketh me to lie
down in green pastures: he leadeth me beside the still waters.
He restoreth my soul. . .
PSALM 23:1–3 KJV

I will find my rest in God alone. He is the One who gives me hope.
PSALM 62:5 NIrV

*Rest is an internal state of soul, a relaxing into God's chest even when
dashing through a day or a season.*
JANE RUBIETTA

Come to Me, all you who labor and are heavy laden, and I will
give you rest. Take My yoke upon you and learn from Me, for I am
gentle and lowly in heart, and you will find rest for your souls.
MATTHEW 11:28–29 NKJV

Only people who have faith will enter the place of rest.
HEBREWS 4:3 CEV

# 56

*Revenge*

Many people assume that not taking revenge is a New Testament concept. After all, didn't Jesus surprise His listeners by saying that if someone slapped their right cheek, to offer them the other cheek also?

Wasn't the rule in the Old Testament "an eye for an eye, and a tooth for a tooth"?

Yes, it was. But it was up to the courts to exact the retribution or the monetary reimbursement. God's people were to step back and let the justice system do its job.

God commanded His people not to try to get revenge— nor to lie in court to get back at someone for a past slight.

Jesus took this a step further: we are to love those who have wronged us. That attitude will keep us from seeking revenge for offenses—whether serious or petty.

We are to trust that God is a God of justice, and in the end He will punish those who have done evil. In the meantime, we are to love.

Simeon and Levi are two of a kind, ready to fight at the drop of a hat. I don't want anything to do with their vendettas, want no part in their bitter feuds; they kill men in fits of temper, slash oxen on a whim.
GENESIS 49:5 MSG

Do not try to get even. Do not hold anything against one of your people. Instead, love your neighbor as you love yourself. I am the Lord.
LEVITICUS 19:18 NIrV

Do not testify against your neighbor without cause—would you use your lips to mislead? Do not say, "I'll do to them as they have done to me; I'll pay them back for what they did."
PROVERBS 24:28–29 NIV

> *Returning evil for evil is the childish attitude of*
> *"he did this to me so I'll do this to him."*
> JO BERRY

Don't insist on getting even; that's not for you to do. "I'll do the judging," says God. "I'll take care of it." Our Scriptures tell us that if you see your enemy hungry, go buy that person lunch, or if he's thirsty, get him a drink. Your generosity will surprise him with goodness. Don't let evil get the best of you; get the best of evil by doing good.
ROMANS 12:18–21 MSG

> *Forgiveness allows us to lay aside the riddles of retribution and human*
> *fairness, and to experience true peace of heart.*
> JOHANN CHRISTOPH ARNOLD

And will not God give justice to his elect, who cry to him day and night? Will he delay long over them? I tell you, he will give justice to them speedily.
LUKE 18:7–8 ESV

And to you who are troubled rest with us, when the Lord Jesus shall be revealed from heaven with his mighty angels, in flaming fire taking vengeance on them that know not God, and that obey not the gospel of our Lord Jesus Christ.
2 THESSALONIANS 1:7–8 KJV

Do not rejoice when your enemy falls, and do not let your heart be glad when he stumbles; or the LORD will see it and be displeased, and turn His anger away from him.
PROVERBS 24:17–18 NASB

*A revengeful spirit is contrary to our heavenly calling.*
THOMAS MANTON

Love your enemies, bless them that curse you, do good to them that hate you, and pray for them which despitefully use you, and persecute you.
MATTHEW 5:44 KJV

Do not do wrong to repay a wrong, and do not insult to repay an insult. But repay with a blessing, because you yourselves were called to do this so that you might receive a blessing.
1 PETER 3:9 NCV

See that no one renders evil for evil to anyone, but always pursue what is good both for yourselves and for all.
1 THESSALONIANS 5:15 NKJV

# 57

## Salvation

Salvation means to be saved from danger. In the Old Testament, salvation was understood to mean Israel being delivered from her enemies. But by Jesus' day, the Jews realized that they needed to be set free from sin as well.

We have all sinned, and the punishment for sin is death—not merely physical death, but spiritual death, eternal separation from God.

No matter how righteous we try to be, no matter how many good deeds we do, our own "works of righteousness" can never save us from hell. We can't earn salvation.

God therefore sent His Son, Jesus, to die on a cross to pay the penalty for our sin. He died in our place because of His great love for us. In so doing, He "ransomed" us with His blood. All we have to do is repent of our sins, believe in Him, and we're saved.

There are not different paths to God. Jesus is the only One who can save us.

Because all people have sinned,
they have fallen short of God's glory.
ROMANS 3:23 GW

When you sin, the pay you get is death. But God gives you the gift of eternal life because of what Christ Jesus our Lord has done.
ROMANS 6:23 NIrv

For God so loved the world that He gave His only begotten Son, that whoever believes in Him should not perish but have everlasting life.
JOHN 3:16 NKJV

Salvation is found in no one else, for there is no other name under heaven given to mankind by which we must be saved.
ACTS 4:12 NIV

*The only thing of our very own which we contribute to our salvation is the sin which makes it necessary.*
WILLIAM TEMPLE

If you declare with your mouth, "Jesus is Lord," and believe in your heart that God raised him from the dead, you will be saved. For it is with your heart that you believe and are justified, and it is with your mouth that you profess your faith and are saved.
ROMANS 10:9–10 TNIV

For by grace you have been saved through faith. And this is not your own doing; it is the gift of God, not a result of works, so that no one may boast.
EPHESIANS 2:8–9 ESV

*When you truly believe what the Bible says about Jesus Christ and decide to follow Him, to let Him be your Master, something miraculous happens.*
KAY ARTHUR

As God's partners, we beg you not to accept this marvelous gift of God's kindness and then ignore it. For God says, "At just the right time, I heard you. On the day of salvation, I helped you." Indeed, the "right time" is now. Today is the day of salvation.
2 CORINTHIANS 6:1–2 NLT

*Those who genuinely cry out to the Lord for salvation are instantly born again by the Spirit of God, who then dwells forever within them.*
BILL GOTHARD

And inasmuch as it is appointed for men to die once and after this comes judgment, so Christ also, having been offered once to bear the sins of many, will appear a second time for salvation without reference to sin, to those who eagerly await Him.
HEBREWS 9:27–28 NASB

Like newborn babies, crave pure spiritual milk, so that by it you may grow up in your salvation, now that you have tasted that the Lord is good.
1 PETER 2:2–3 NIV

And you also were included in Christ when you heard the message of truth, the gospel of your salvation. When you believed, you were marked in him with a seal, the promised Holy Spirit, who is a deposit guaranteeing our inheritance until the redemption of those who are God's possession.
EPHESIANS 1:13–14 NIV

# 58

*selflessness*

For many of us, before we were Christians, our lives were full of selfish living and looking out for number one. We were in it for what we could get for ourselves. Even if we weren't hedonistic party animals, we still spent our money to gratify our desires.

But when the Spirit of Christ entered our heart, it made a difference: we began to move from being self-centered to being Christ-centered.

Rather than continuing to live according to a "me first" philosophy, we are now to love others as much as we love ourselves.

This transformation takes time, however. Selfishness is a fundamental part of our sinful human nature, and our old self constantly wants to reestablish its supremacy. This is why we must continually say no to selfish desires.

Jesus was the ultimate example of a man living a selfless life, and as His disciples we are to emulate Him. As we follow in His footsteps, we become true men of God.

But mark this: There will be terrible times in the last days.
People will be lovers of themselves.
2 TIMOTHY 3:1–2 NIV

Your life on earth was full of rich living and pleasing yourselves with everything you wanted.
JAMES 5:5 NCV

A person who isn't friendly looks out only for himself.
He opposes all good sense.
PROVERBS 18:1 NIrV

*Individuals motivated by self-interest, self-indulgence,
and a false sense of self-sufficiency pursue selfish ambition
for the purpose of self-glorification.*
C. J. MAHANEY

But if you have bitter jealousy and selfish ambition in your hearts,
do not boast and be false to the truth. This is not the wisdom
that comes down from above, but is earthly, unspiritual, demonic.
JAMES 3:14–15 ESV

They are looking for profits and do not control
their selfish desires.
PSALM 73:7 NCV

*You were designed to love. That's where your happiness lies—
not in an endless chase after selfish pleasures.*
CLAIRE AND CURT CLONINGER

Let each of you look out not only for his own interests,
but also for the interests of others.
PHILIPPIANS 2:4 NKJV

Love cares more for others than for self. Love doesn't want what
it doesn't have. Love doesn't strut, doesn't have a swelled head,
doesn't force itself on others, isn't always "me first."
1 CORINTHIANS 13:4–5 MSG

I have no one else like Timothy. He truly cares about how you
are doing. All the others are looking out for their own interests.
They are not looking out for the interests of Jesus Christ.
PHILIPPIANS 2:20–21 NIRV

*One sign of spiritual immaturity is to be selfish;*
*a sign of maturity is to be selfless.*
JILL BRISCOE

Live freely, animated and motivated by God's Spirit. Then you won't feed the compulsions of selfishness. For there is a root of sinful self-interest in us that is at odds with a free spirit, just as the free spirit is incompatible with selfishness.
GALATIANS 5:16 MSG

Then Jesus said to his disciples, "If any of you wants to be my follower, you must turn from your selfish ways, take up your cross, and follow me."
MATTHEW 16:24 NLT

# 59

## self-sufficiency

Pride is one of the most common faults to beset men, and one way it manifests itself is in a spirit of self-sufficiency and independence.

This may come as a surprise to many of us. After all, we know that the Bible says we are to work hard to earn our own living so that we won't have to depend upon others.

No, we shouldn't depend upon others. But we should depend upon God.

The attitude the Bible warns us to guard against is that of the "self-made man," the man who's confident in his ability to make his own way through life—who thinks that he alone deserves credit for his successes.

We may have been born with drive, business savvy, and talents, but many ambitious, savvy, talented men never achieve lasting success. Without God's blessing, we will fail.

Even if we manage to succeed on a material level, without God we're miserable and our victories are meaningless. We need to realize how much we depend on God.

"Beware that you do not forget the LORD your God. . .lest—when you have eaten and are full, and have built beautiful houses and dwell in them; and when your herds and your flocks multiply, and your silver and your gold are multiplied, and all that you have is multiplied; when your heart is lifted up, and you forget the LORD your God. . .then you say in your heart, 'My power and the might of my hand have gained me this wealth.' And you shall remember the LORD your God, for it is He who gives you power to get wealth."
DEUTERONOMY 8:11–14, 17–18 NKJV

*What is pride? Pride is rooted in self-dependency and self-focus.*
*Pride can be strutting our stuff: "I don't need God.*
*I can do this on my own."*
CHIP INGRAM

This is what the LORD says: "Let not the wise man boast of their wisdom or the strong boast of their strength or the rich boast of their riches, but let the one who boasts boast about this: that they have the understanding to know me, that I am the LORD."
JEREMIAH 9:23–24 NIV

Cursed is the man who trusts in man and makes flesh his strength, whose heart turns away from the LORD.
JEREMIAH 17:5 ESV

*Remember the wealthy farmer of Jesus' parable, who essentially*
*boasted, "I've got it made"? (See Luke 12:13–21.) It didn't*
*turn out well. Do all your bragging on God.*

So Uzziah became famous in faraway places, because he had much help until he became powerful. But when Uzziah became powerful, his pride led to his ruin.
2 CHRONICLES 26:15–16 NCV

I will go in the strength of the Lord GOD: I will make mention of thy righteousness, even of thine only.
PSALM 71:16 KJV

*Begin your day by acknowledging your dependence*
*upon God and your need for God.*
C. J. MAHANEY

I am the vine. You are the branches. If anyone remains joined to me, and I to him, he will bear a lot of fruit. You can't do anything without me.

JOHN 15:5 NIrV

Not that we are adequate in ourselves to consider anything as coming from ourselves, but our adequacy is from God.

2 CORINTHIANS 3:5 NASB

For I can do everything through Christ, who gives me strength.

PHILIPPIANS 4:13 NLT

# 60

*Service*

As we grow in our Christian faith, we begin to move out from a self-centered life into a life centered on loving and serving God.

And one of the most tangible ways we prove that we love God is by loving and serving others. After all, if we don't love God's children whom we have seen, how can we love God whom we can't see?

Fellow believers are the Body of Christ on earth, so any good deeds we do for others, we are literally doing for Jesus Himself.

Jesus put a large emphasis on Christians serving one another. This means responding to others' needs with acts of service— by cheerfully volunteering and helping out. This is what the expression "having a servant's heart" means.

We may seem to be losing by sacrificially investing time in others, but that's only from a self-centered perspective. Our lives are actually deeply enriched by serving others.

Besides, God has promised to greatly reward us for the good we do.

"Whoever wants to become first among you must serve the rest of you like a slave. In the same way, the Son of Man did not come to be served. He came to serve others."
MATTHEW 20:27–28 NCV

> *What is the kingdom of Christ? A rule of love, of truth—*
> *a rule of service. The king is the chief servant in it.*
> GEORGE MacDONALD

You should think in the same way Christ Jesus does. . . .
He made himself nothing. He took on the very nature of a servant.
PHILIPPIANS 2:5, 7 NIrV

In Joppa there was a disciple named Tabitha (in Greek her name is Dorcas); she was always doing good and helping the poor. . . . All the widows stood around him, crying and showing him the robes and other clothing that Dorcas had made while she was still with them.
ACTS 9:36, 39 TNIV

So then, as we have opportunity, let us do good to everyone, and especially to those who are of the household of faith.
GALATIANS 6:10 ESV

*One of the most powerful ways to gain entrance into someone's heart is to serve them.*
MELODY ROSSI

For you, brethren, have been called to liberty; only do not use liberty as an opportunity for the flesh, but through love serve one another.
GALATIANS 5:13 NKJV

Each of you should use whatever gift you have received to serve others, as faithful stewards of God's grace in its various forms.
1 PETER 4:10 NIV

Whatever you do, work at it with all your heart, as working for the Lord, not for human masters, since you know that you will receive an inheritance from the Lord as a reward. It is the Lord Christ you are serving.
COLOSSIANS 3:23–24 NIV

*One can so easily become too great to be used by God. One can never be too small for His service.*
CORRIE TEN BOOM

*Christians in their effectual calling, are not called to idleness, but to labor in God's vineyard, and spend their day in doing a great and laborious service.*

JONATHAN EDWARDS

For God is not unrighteous to forget your work and labour of love, which ye have shewed toward his name, in that ye have ministered to the saints, and do minister.
HEBREWS 6:10 KJV

You know, they were among the first converts in Greece, and they've put themselves out, serving Christians ever since then. I want you to honor and look up to people like that: companions and workers who show us how to do it, giving us something to aspire to.
1 CORINTHIANS 16:15–16 MSG

And let us not be weary in well doing: for in due season we shall reap, if we faint not.
GALATIANS 6:9 KJV

# 61

*Sin*

We have all sinned. Perhaps we have difficulty accepting that if we haven't committed large, serious sins, but we have sinned nonetheless—and not just on rare occasions. It's in our very nature, inherited from Adam.

We have all been guilty of so-called minor sins like pride, selfishness, envy, backbiting, lying, lust, etc.

The Greek word for "sin" means "to miss the mark," and we've all done that.

The sobering news is that sin has serious consequences—spiritual death. The good news is that Jesus, God's Son, paid the price for our sin. If we confess that we are sinners who need to be forgiven, and ask God to forgive us, He takes our sins away.

From then on when He looks at us, God sees the righteousness of Christ—not our sinful nature. Our sins are covered by the blood of Christ.

God also sends the Spirit of His Son into our lives to help us obey Him and no longer give in to sin.

For there is not a just man on earth who does good
and does not sin.
ECCLESIASTES 7:20 NKJV

If we say that we have no sin, we deceive ourselves,
and the truth is not in us.
1 JOHN 1:8 KJV

Sin entered the world because one man sinned. And death came
because of sin. Everyone sinned, so death came to all people.
ROMANS 5:12–13 NIrV

*Sin is wrong, not because of what it does to me, or my spouse,*
*or child, or neighbor, but because it is an act of rebellion*
*against the infinitely holy and majestic God.*
JERRY BRIDGES

Jesus replied, "I tell you the truth, everyone who sins
is a slave of sin."
JOHN 8:34 NLT

For while we were living in the flesh, our sinful passions, aroused
by the law, were at work in our members to bear fruit for death.
ROMANS 7:5 ESV

For as in Adam all die, so in Christ all will be made alive.
1 CORINTHIANS 15:22 TNIV

*After grief for sin there should be joy for forgiveness.*
A. W. PINK

[Jesus] himself bore our sins in his body on the tree, that we
might die to sin and live to righteousness. By his wounds you
have been healed.
1 PETER 2:24 ESV

For He made Him who knew no sin to be sin for us, that we
might become the righteousness of God in Him.
2 CORINTHIANS 5:21 NKJV

The next day [John the Baptist] saw Jesus coming toward him,
and said, "Behold, the Lamb of God, who takes away the
sin of the world!"
JOHN 1:29 ESV

*It does not spoil your happiness to confess your sin.*
*The unhappiness is in not making the confession.*
CHARLES H. SPURGEON

If we confess our sins, he is faithful and just to forgive us our sins, and to cleanse us from all unrighteousness.
1 JOHN 1:9 KJV

When [Jesus] died, he died once to break the power of sin. But now that he lives, he lives for the glory of God. So you also should consider yourselves to be dead to the power of sin and alive to God through Christ Jesus. Do not let sin control the way you live; do not give in to sinful desires.
ROMANS 6:10–12 NLT

No one who abides in him keeps on sinning; no one who keeps on sinning has either seen him or known him.
1 JOHN 3:6 ESV

*We must learn where our personal weaknesses lie. Once they are*
*identified, we must be ruthless in dealing with them.*
ALISTAIR BEGG

Therefore, dear brothers and sisters, you have no obligation to do what your sinful nature urges you to do. For if you live by its dictates, you will die. But if through the power of the Spirit you put to death the deeds of your sinful nature, you will live.
ROMANS 8:12–13 NLT

# 62

## Spiritual Fruit

Paul wrote that "the fruit of the Spirit is love, joy, peace, forbearance, kindness, goodness, faithfulness, gentleness and self-control" (Galatians 5:22–23 NIV).

Why did he call these virtues "the fruit of the Spirit"?

Well, remember that Jesus said in John 15 that He is the grapevine and we are the branches. A vine's branches are alive only as long as they're attached to the vine. Just as the sap of the grapevine gives the branches life, so Jesus' Spirit gives us spiritual life.

But when the Spirit lives in you He does more than simply give you eternal life. The Spirit also invariably causes you to develop and manifest Christian virtues.

As Jesus said in Matthew 7, the good fruit is the ultimate proof that you belong to Him.

We don't cause virtues to grow through our own human effort. That's the job of the Holy Spirit. But our job is to stay connected to the vine and let Him work in us.

Remain in me, as I also remain in you. No branch can bear fruit by itself; it must remain in the vine. Neither can you bear fruit unless you remain in me. I am the vine; you are the branches. If you remain in me and I in you, you will bear much fruit; apart from me you can do nothing.
JOHN 15:4–5 NIV

But the fruit of the Spirit is love, joy, peace, longsuffering, kindness, goodness, faithfulness, gentleness, self-control. Against such there is no law.
GALATIANS 5:22–23 NKJV

*The fruit of the Spirit is not push, drive, climb, grasp and trample. . . .*
*Life is more than a climb to the top of the heap.*
RICHARD J. FOSTER

You can identify them by their fruit, that is, by the way they act.
Can you pick grapes from thornbushes, or figs from thistles?
A good tree produces good fruit, and a bad tree produces bad fruit.
MATTHEW 7:16–17 NLT

Likewise, my brothers, you also have died to the law through the
body of Christ, so that you may belong to another, to him who
has been raised from the dead, in order that we may bear
fruit for God.
ROMANS 7:4 ESV

For you were once darkness, but now you are light in the Lord.
Live as children of light (for the fruit of the light consists in all
goodness, righteousness and truth) and find out what
pleases the Lord.
EPHESIANS 5:8 10 NIV

*The fruit of the Spirit is about our character, not our behavior or*
*conduct. The fruit of the Spirit is about being not doing.*
MICHAEL YOUSSEF

I pray that your love will overflow more and more, and that you
will keep on growing in knowledge and understanding. For I
want you to understand what really matters, so that you may live
pure and blameless lives until the day of Christ's return. May you
always be filled with the fruit of your salvation—the righteous
character produced in your life by Jesus Christ—for this will bring
much glory and praise to God.
PHILIPPIANS 1:9–11 NLT

[And we pray this] so that you may live a life worthy of the Lord and please him in every way: bearing fruit in every good work, growing in the knowledge of God.

COLOSSIANS 1:10 NIV

*God develops the fruit of the Spirit in your life by allowing you to experience circumstances in which you're tempted to express the exact opposite quality. Character development always involves a choice, and temptation provides that opportunity.*

RICK WARREN

Blessed is the one who does not walk in step with the wicked or stand in the way that sinners take or sit in the company of mockers, but whose delight is in the law of the LORD, and who meditates on his law day and night. That person is like a tree planted by streams of water, which yields its fruit in season and whose leaf does not wither—whatever they do prospers.

PSALM 1:1–3 NIV

# 63

## Spiritual Gifts

Each one of us is a unique creation of God, designed for a special purpose in life. God built special talents and abilities right into your DNA. He might have made you a gifted speaker, a detail man, a singer, an athlete, or have given you great organizational skills.

These gifts were given to you at conception, long before you became a Christian. But spiritual gifts—"the gifts of the Spirit"—are extra gifts you receive after salvation.

The Holy Spirit gives all of us eternal life and develops Christlike virtues in all of us, but the spiritual gifts He gives are unique, each one tailored to His plan for our life. Read the following lists and see which spiritual gifts you have.

If you don't think you have any of them, ask God to give you one.

Just remember, these gifts aren't given just for your individual benefit. God gives them to you so that you can help and strengthen other Christians.

Now there are varieties of gifts, but the same Spirit.
1 CORINTHIANS 12:4–5 ESV

But the manifestation of the Spirit is given to each one for the profit of all: for to one is given the word of wisdom through the Spirit, to another the word of knowledge through the same Spirit, to another faith by the same Spirit, to another gifts of healings by the same Spirit, to another the working of miracles, to another prophecy, to another discerning of spirits, to another different kinds of tongues, to another the interpretation of tongues. But one and the same Spirit works all these things, distributing to each one individually as He wills.
1 CORINTHIANS 12:7–11 NKJV

*Your spiritual gifts were not given for your own benefit but for the benefit of others just as other people were given gifts for your benefit.*
RICK WARREN

For I say, through the grace given to me, to everyone who is among you, not to think of himself more highly than he ought to think, but to think soberly, as God has dealt to each one a measure of faith. For as we have many members in one body, but all the members do not have the same function, so we, being many, are one body in Christ, and individually members of one another. Having then gifts differing according to the grace that is given to us, let us use them: if prophecy, let us prophesy in proportion to our faith; or ministry, let us use it in our ministering; he who teaches, in teaching; he who exhorts, in exhortation; he who gives, with liberality; he who leads, with diligence; he who shows mercy, with cheerfulness.
ROMANS 12:3–8 NKJV

*Do you have spiritual gifts and treasures that you have put into storage and are not using? Give them away, clear the closet!*
KATHERINE WALDEN

And God has placed in the church first of all apostles, second prophets, third teachers, then miracles, then gifts of healing, of helping, of guidance, and of different kinds of tongues.
1 CORINTHIANS 12:28 NIV

So what makes us think we can escape if we ignore this great salvation that was first announced by the Lord Jesus himself and then delivered to us by those who heard him speak? And God confirmed the message by giving signs and wonders and various miracles and gifts of the Holy Spirit whenever he chose.
HEBREWS 2:3–4 NLT

*If we seek the gifts of the Spirit and not the Holy Spirit Himself, we'll always focus on self. We must learn to understand that there are no gifts apart from an intimate relationship with the Spirit.*

HENRY AND MEL BLACKABY

Pursue love, and earnestly desire the spiritual gifts, especially that you may prophesy.

1 CORINTHIANS 14:1 ESV

# 64

## Sports

Many men enjoy participating in some kind of sport—and they could hardly do anything better for their health. Sports also teach good things like teamwork, obeying the rules, discipline, and focus.

Sports are also exciting, fascinating, and just plain enjoyable. For many men, they're as fun to watch as they are to participate in.

Women who think that men don't know how to show their emotions have never been present when a tied game is broken by a goal in overtime.

The apostle Paul used a lot of sports references in his letters to the churches—he described wrestlers, boxers, and runners, and probably would have included baseball, basketball, and football players if those games had existed in his time.

But even though playing sports is a competitive endeavor, Paul wasn't urging his readers to defeat the next guy. He simply wanted the followers of Jesus to play by the rules, to work hard, to strive to better themselves.

So what's your favorite sport?

So, Jeremiah, if you're worn out in this footrace with men, what makes you think you can race against horses?
JEREMIAH 12:5 MSG

Moses was educated in the best schools in Egypt. He was equally impressive as a thinker and an athlete.
ACTS 7:22 MSG

For we wrestle not against flesh and blood, but against principalities, against powers, against the rulers of the darkness of this world, against spiritual wickedness in high places.
EPHESIANS 6:12 KJV

*You decide each day whether you will run the race in such a way
as to get the prize or limp along in a halfhearted effort.*
HARRY R. JACKSON

You know that many runners enter a race, and only one of them
wins the prize. So run to win!
1 CORINTHIANS 9:24 CEV

Everyone who competes in the games goes into strict training.
They do it to get a crown that will not last, but we do it to get a
crown that will last forever.
1 CORINTHIANS 9:25 NIV

Therefore I do not run like one who runs aimlessly,
or box like one who beats the air.
1 CORINTHIANS 9:26 HCSB

You were running a good race. Who stopped you from
following the true way?
GALATIANS 5:7 NCV

I discipline my body like an athlete, training it to do what it
should. Otherwise, I fear that after preaching to others I myself
might be disqualified.
1 CORINTHIANS 9:27 NLT

*Nice guys may appear to finish last but usually
they are running in a different race.*
KEN BLANCHARD

Similarly, anyone who competes as an athlete does not receive
the victor's crown except by competing according to the rules.
2 TIMOTHY 2:5 NIV

Therefore, since we are surrounded by such a huge crowd of witnesses to the life of faith, let us strip off every weight that slows us down, especially the sin that so easily trips us up. And let us run with endurance the race God has set before us.
HEBREWS 12:1 NLT

> *The Christian life was intended not to be a sitting still,*
> *but a race, a perpetual motion.*
> CHARLES H. SPURGEON

This is the only race worth running. I've run hard right to the finish, believed all the way. All that's left now is the shouting— God's applause!
2 TIMOTHY 4:6 MSG

I have fought the good fight, I have finished the race, and I have remained faithful.
2 TIMOTHY 4:7 NLT

# 65

## Stress

We're not the first generation to have to deal with a seemingly unrelenting barrage of pressure on our lives. The Bible talks repeatedly about stress and distress, which shows that mankind has been dealing with it for thousands of years.

Even Bible greats like David suffered anxiety, and the apostle Paul was so hemmed in and weighed down at times that he had to fight giving in to despair.

Prophets like Elijah and Jonah suffered bouts of depression.

We sometimes bring stress upon ourselves by taking on too much responsibility. Often we cause ourselves grief because of wrong choices. But just as often stress comes upon us due to unforeseen calamities and financial disasters.

Whatever its source, stress can be debilitating. It can either break us or drive us to our knees in prayer—and like King David, our prayers may consist largely of tears and groaning.

But God hears and answers such prayers. He did for David, and He will for us.

Anxiety in the heart of man causes depression,
but a good word makes it glad.
PROVERBS 12:25 NKJV

Delayed hope makes the heart sick,
but fulfilled desire is a tree of life.
PROVERBS 13:12 HCSB

*Adversity—It can drive us to our knees in despair and depression*
*or it can drive us to our knees in humble recognition of our*
*dependence on the Father. It's our choice.*
REBECCA LUSIGNOLO-MCGLONE

But understand this, that in the last days there will come times of difficulty.
2 TIMOTHY 3:1 ESV

"The seed cast in the weeds represents the ones who hear the kingdom news but are overwhelmed with worries about all the things they have to do and all the things they want to get. The stress strangles what they heard, and nothing comes of it.
MARK 4:18 MSG

Greedy people want everything and are never satisfied. But when nothing remains for them to grab, they will be nothing. Once they have everything, distress and despair will strike them down.
JOB 20:20–22 CEV

*Poor choices whether morally, relationally or spiritually lead to unrest, stress and anxiety.*
JOHN DEMARCO

Having them to share the load will make your work easier. This is the way God wants it done. You won't be under nearly as much stress, and everyone else will return home feeling satisfied.
EXODUS 18:22–23 CEV

As pressure and stress bear down on me,
I find joy in your commands.
PSALM 119:143 NLT

*Anger and bitterness are misplaced responses when you understand that when "the worst thing that could happen" happens, God is still there.*
STAN GUTHRIE

We are hard pressed on every side, but not crushed; perplexed, but not in despair; persecuted, but not abandoned; struck down, but not destroyed.
2 CORINTHIANS 4:8–9 NIV

I am numb and completely devastated. I roar because my heart's in turmoil. You know all my desires, O Lord, and my groaning has not been hidden from you.
PSALM 38:8–9 GW

Answer me when I call to you, my righteous God. Give me relief from my distress; have mercy on me and hear my prayer.
PSALM 4:1 NIV

*He only that stills the stormy seas,*
*can quiet the distressed and tempestuous soul.*
JOHN FLAVEL

In my distress I called upon the LORD, and cried out to my God; He heard my voice from His temple, and my cry came before Him, even to His ears.
PSALM 18:6 NKJV

I am leaving you with a gift—peace of mind and heart. And the peace I give is a gift the world cannot give. So don't be troubled or afraid.
JOHN 14:27 NLT

# 66

*Success*

When we think of a "successful" man, the first image that comes to mind is a man who has a good-paying job, owns a nice home, is happily married, and has obedient children. We wish such success for ourselves!

But if his marriage breaks down or his children rebel, we question how successful he is, even though he has a terrific job and home.

We should question even more the success and prosperity of a man who has everything that this world has to offer, but who places no value on his own soul.

Prosperity is good, and it's nice to have everything in life turn out great—and God sometimes blesses His people with these things—but success can't be defined only as material gain. After all, Jesus said, "Blessed are the poor."

It's more important to prosper spiritually even if we're not wealthy. It's more important to successfully follow God than it is to succeed in business.

May God help us to truly succeed and prosper.

Only be strong and very courageous; be careful to do according to all the law which Moses My servant commanded you; do not turn from it to the right or to the left, so that you may have success wherever you go. This book of the law shall not depart from your mouth, but you shall meditate on it day and night, so that you may be careful to do according to all that is written in it; for then you will make your way prosperous, and then you will have success.

JOSHUA 1:7–8 NASB

*There are great positives as well as refusals necessary for him who would find real prosperity. He must not only say no to the wrong, he must say yes to the right. He must not only avoid the seat of the scornful, but his delight must be in the law of the Lord.*

CLOVIS G. CHAPPELL

Blessed is the one who does not walk in step with the wicked or stand in the way that sinners take or sit in the company of mockers, but whose delight is in the law of the LORD, and who meditates on his law day and night. That person is like a tree planted by streams of water, which yields its fruit in season and whose leaf does not wither—whatever they do prospers.

PSALM 1:1–3 NIV

The LORD was with Joseph so that he prospered, and he lived in the house of his Egyptian master. When his master saw that the LORD was with him and that the LORD gave him success in everything he did, Joseph found favor in his eyes and became his attendant.

GENESIS 39:2–4 NIV

*External criteria such as affluence, numbers, money, or positive response have never been the biblical measure of success in ministry. Faithfulness, godliness, and spiritual commitment are the virtues God esteems.*

JOHN MACARTHUR

[King Hezekiah] trusted in the LORD, the God of Israel, so that there was none like him among all the kings of Judah after him, nor among those who were before him. For he held fast to the LORD. He did not depart from following him, but kept the commandments that the LORD commanded Moses. And the LORD was with him; wherever he went out, he prospered.

2 KINGS 18:5–7 ESV

*Before Nehemiah spoke to King Artaxerxes about rebuilding Jerusalem,*
*he prayed for success in bringing his case before the king. There is*
*nothing we cannot ask God for, as long as we are seeking His will.*

Lord, let your ear be attentive to the prayer of this your servant
and to the prayer of your servants who delight in revering your
name. Give your servant success today by granting him favor in
the presence of this man.
NEHEMIAH 1:11 NIV

Save now, I pray, O LORD; O LORD, I pray, send now prosperity.
PSALM 118:25 NKJV

He who conceals his transgressions will not prosper, but he who
confesses and forsakes them will find compassion.
PROVERBS 28:13 NASB

*We must teach our children that the real measure of their success in life*
*is how much they'd be worth if they had absolutely nothing.*
WALT MUELLER

Beloved, I pray that you may prosper in all things and be in
health, just as your soul prospers.
3 JOHN 1:2 NKJV

For what will it profit a man if he gains the whole world,
and loses his own soul?
MARK 8:36 NKJV

David continued to succeed in everything he did,
for the LORD was with him.
1 SAMUEL 18:14 NLT

# 67

## Teamwork

Having the humility to submit to a team captain or follow a leader's orders is one thing. At least you know he's the boss. He has clearly designated authority.

Working together with the rest of the team, however—people who are more or less on equal footing as you—can present special challenges.

Certain individuals can be particularly trying. You just naturally clash with some personality types, especially if they try to boss you around or insist on doing things their way—which, as far as you can see, is the wrong way.

Yet without a team working efficiently together, getting along, with each member doing his part, the job won't get done well, on time—or even at all.

Christians are the Body of Christ, and it is mandatory that each part of a body do its designated task, not working cross-purposes to the rest of the members. Otherwise God's purposes won't be accomplished.

Unity, humility, and mutual respect are essential when working together.

So all the Israelites got together and united as one against the city.
JUDGES 20:11 NIV

Join together in following my example, brothers and sisters, and just as you have us as a model, keep your eyes on those who live as we do.
PHILIPPIANS 3:17 NIV

And further, submit to one another out of reverence for Christ.
EPHESIANS 5:21 NLT

I want you to honor and look up to people like that: companions and workers who show us how to do it, giving us something to aspire to.
1 CORINTHIANS 16:16 MSG

*The least important word: I—it gets the least amount done.*
*The most important word: we—it gets the most amount done.*
JOHN C. MAXWELL

Likewise you younger people, submit yourselves to your elders. Yes, all of you be submissive to one another, and be clothed with humility, for "God resists the proud, but gives grace to the humble."
1 PETER 5:5 NKJV

I appeal to you, brothers, by the name of our Lord Jesus Christ, that all of you agree, and that there be no divisions among you, but that you be united in the same mind and the same judgment.
1 CORINTHIANS 1:10 ESV

*Unity and diversity must work together or one will destroy the other.*
*Unity without diversity is uniformity, but diversity*
*without unity is anarchy.*
WARREN W. WIERSBE

Apollos and I are merely servants who helped you to have faith. It was the Lord who made it all happen. I planted the seeds, Apollos watered them, but God made them sprout and grow. What matters isn't those who planted or watered, but God who made the plants grow. The one who plants is just as important as the one who waters. And each one will be paid for what they do. Apollos and I work together for God, and you are God's garden and God's building.
1 CORINTHIANS 3:5–9 CEV

But now hath God set the members every one of them in the body, as it hath pleased him. And if they were all one member, where were the body? But now are they many members, yet but one body. And the eye cannot say unto the hand, I have no need of thee: nor again the head to the feet, I have no need of you.
1 CORINTHIANS 12:18–21 KJV

*We must each see ourselves as vital members of the body,*
*each entrusted with the care of the whole.*
JANE WINEBRENNER AND DEBRA FRAZIER

Above all else, you must live in a way that brings honor to the good news about Christ. Then, whether I visit you or not, I will hear that all of you think alike. I will know that you are working together and that you are struggling side by side to get others to believe the good news.
PHILIPPIANS 1:27 CEV

# 68

## *Temptation*

When we think of men being tempted, it's easy to assume that the temptation is sexual in nature, but that's only one area men are tempted in. Consider when Jesus was tempted.

First the devil tempted Him to prove His power by turning stones into bread. We, too, are tempted in pride to show off our strength or ability.

Then the devil tried to trick Jesus into taking a foolhardy risk, presuming upon God's promise to protect Him.

Finally, Satan offered Jesus all the kingdoms of this world if Jesus would worship him. We, too, are tempted to compromise our faith for riches, power, and glory.

Jesus was tempted in every possible area a man can be tempted in, but He never caved in. He overcame each temptation by quoting and obeying the Word of God.

Jesus knows our areas of weakness and has sent His Spirit into our heart to strengthen us, to help us make the right choice, and to stick to it.

Then Jesus was led up by the Spirit into the wilderness to be tempted by the devil. And after fasting forty days and forty nights, he was hungry. And the tempter came and said to him, "If you are the Son of God, command these stones to become loaves of bread." But he answered, "It is written, 'Man shall not live by bread alone, but by every word that comes from the mouth of God.'"

Matthew 4:1–4 ESV

*Follow Jesus' example the next time you're faced with temptation. Remember what you know of God's Word, then ask God to help you fight the battle.*

Greg Laurie

After the devil had finished tempting Jesus in every possible way, the devil left him until another time.
LUKE 4:13 GW

Because he himself suffered when he was tempted, he is able to help those who are being tempted.
HEBREWS 2:18 TNIV

For our high priest is able to understand our weaknesses.
He was tempted in every way that we are, but he did not sin.
HEBREWS 4:15 NCV

No temptation has overtaken you except what is common to humanity. God is faithful and He will not allow you to be tempted beyond what you are able, but with the temptation He will also provide a way of escape, so that you are able to bear it.
1 CORINTHIANS 10:13 HCSB

*All we need do is obey the words of Jesus and abide in that Word and we'll have an answer for any lie or temptation Satan throws our way.*
TONY EVANS

When tempted, no one should say, "God is tempting me." For God cannot be tempted by evil, nor does he tempt anyone; but each person is tempted when they are dragged away by their own evil desire and enticed.
JAMES 1:13–14 NIV

Keep us from falling into sin when we are tempted.
Save us from the evil one.
MATTHEW 6:13 NIrV

Watch and pray so that you will not fall into temptation.
The spirit is willing, but the flesh is weak.
MATTHEW 26:41 TNIV

> *Tomorrow's character is made out of today's thoughts.*
> *Temptation may come suddenly, but sin doesn't.*
> RANDY ALCORN

For this reason, when I could no longer endure it, I sent to know
your faith, lest by some means the tempter had tempted you,
and our labor might be in vain.
1 THESSALONIANS 3:5 NKJV

People who want to be rich fall into all sorts of temptations and
traps. They are caught by foolish and harmful desires that drag
them down and destroy them.
1 TIMOTHY 6:9 CEV

> *You are free to choose what you surrender to,*
> *but you are not free from the consequences of that choice.*
> RICK WARREN

Blessed is the man that endureth temptation: for when he is tried,
he shall receive the crown of life, which the Lord hath promised
to them that love him.
JAMES 1:12 KJV

Brothers and sisters, if someone is caught in a sin, you who
live by the Spirit should restore that person gently. But watch
yourselves, or you also may be tempted.
GALATIANS 6:1 NIV

# 69

## The Poor

People are poor for many reasons: one of the most common is that they were born into poverty and raised in an impoverished nation with few resources.

America has long been seen as a land of opportunity— a nation built by poor immigrants who, through hard work and ingenuity, made a better life—so we often tend to think that hard work alone is the solution to poverty.

Often this is correct.

But hundreds of millions of laborers around the world work very hard and are still poor. Even in our own land, millions struggle to pay their bills and buy food. Jobs are scarce.

Poverty won't go away by ignoring it. Jesus said, "You will always have the poor among you" (Mark 14:7 NLT), and He therefore urged His followers to be compassionate and give to the needy.

We are also not to despise the poor or deny them justice. God cares for those who have fallen on hard times, and He wants us to care also.

The LORD makes some poor and others rich; he brings some down and lifts others up.
1 SAMUEL 2:7 NLT

*Those who would bring great things to pass must rise early. Love not sleep, lest thou come to poverty.*
MATTHEW HENRY

Good planning and hard work lead to prosperity, but hasty shortcuts lead to poverty.
PROVERBS 21:5 NLT

In all labor there is profit, but idle chatter leads only to poverty.
PROVERBS 14:23 NKJV

A hard worker has plenty of food, but a person who chases
fantasies ends up in poverty.
PROVERBS 28:19 NLT

*Give according to your income, lest God make your income*
*according to your giving.*
OSWALD J. SMITH

Give generously to the poor, not grudgingly, for the LORD your
God will bless you in everything you do. There will always be
some in the land who are poor. That is why I am commanding
you to share freely with the poor and with other
Israelites in need.
DEUTERONOMY 15:10–11 NLT

Those who give to the poor will lack nothing, but those who
close their eyes to them receive many curses.
PROVERBS 28:27 NIV

The generous will themselves be blessed, for they share their
food with the poor.
PROVERBS 22:9 NIV

*A double standard for justice that denies it to the poor is nothing new*
*in this world. God warned against this in His Law,*
*and we still struggle against it today.*

This is what the LORD Almighty said: "Administer true justice; show mercy and compassion to one another. Do not oppress the widow or the fatherless, the foreigner or the poor. Do not plot evil against each other."
ZECHARIAH 7:8–10 NIV

Do not deny justice to your poor people in their lawsuits.
EXODUS 23:6 NIV

You shall do no injustice in judgment; you shall not be partial to the poor nor defer to the great, but you are to judge your neighbor fairly.
LEVITICUS 19:15 NASB

The righteous care about justice for the poor, but the wicked have no such concern.
PROVERBS 29:7 NIV

*The poor man's hand is the treasury of Christ.*
HENRY ALFORD

Then Jesus turned to his disciples and said, "God blesses you who are poor, for the Kingdom of God is yours. God blesses you who are hungry now, for you will be satisfied."
LUKE 6:20–21 NLT

# 70

*Wisdom*

Possessing wisdom is more than being knowledgeable, more than having a head full of facts and figures. Wisdom means having experience and knowledge and applying them judiciously for a good purpose.

The Bible says, however, that even judicious men are not actually wise—not if they reject God and disobey His principles. Better is a "foolish" man who obeys God.

The reason is that God is infinitely wiser than any human. His plans work far better in the long run while "the best laid schemes o' mice an' men gang aft a-gley [often go awry]," to quote Robert Burns. Therefore, any man with the good sense to obey God's commands is wise.

Hence the proverb, "The fear of the LORD is the beginning of wisdom" (Proverbs 1:7 ESV). If we fear God we'll obey Him, and that's wisdom.

It's a good thing if we're intelligent and know how to make judicious, practical decisions based on sound principles, but that's not enough. Those principles must be biblical principles.

Oh, the depth of the riches both of the wisdom and knowledge of God! How unsearchable are His judgments and His ways past finding out!
ROMANS 11:33 NKJV

No wisdom, no understanding, no counsel can avail against the LORD.
PROVERBS 21:30 ESV

*Wisdom [is] an understanding and application of the moral principles of God.*
JERRY BRIDGES

The fear of the LORD is the beginning of wisdom:
and the knowledge of the holy is understanding.
PROVERBS 9:10 KJV

Let no man deceive himself. If any man among you seemeth to
be wise in this world, let him become a fool, that he may be
wise. For the wisdom of this world is foolishness with God. For it
is written, He taketh the wise in their own craftiness. And again,
The Lord knoweth the thoughts of the wise, that they are vain.
1 CORINTHIANS 3:18–20 KJV

Don't be impressed with your own wisdom. Instead, fear the LORD
and turn away from evil.
PROVERBS 3:7 NLT

*There is nothing more foolish than an act of wickedness; there is no
wisdom equal to that of obeying God.*
ALBERT BARNES

Who is wise and understanding among you? Let them show it
by their good life, by deeds done in the humility that
comes from wisdom.
JAMES 3:13 NIV

How blessed is the man who finds wisdom and the man who
gains understanding. For her profit is better than the profit of
silver and her gain better than fine gold.
PROVERBS 3:13–14 NASB

If you need wisdom, ask our generous God, and he will give it to
you. He will not rebuke you for asking.
JAMES 1:5 NLT

*A truly humble man is sensible of his natural distance from God. . .
of the insufficiency of his own power and wisdom. . .and that he needs
God's wisdom to lead and guide him, and His might to enable him to
do what he ought to do for Him.*
JONATHAN EDWARDS

Where there is strife, there is pride, but wisdom is found in
those who take advice.
PROVERBS 13:10 NIV

Listen to advice and accept instruction, that you may gain
wisdom in the future.
PROVERBS 19:20 ESV

But the wisdom from above is first of all pure. It is also peace
loving, gentle at all times, and willing to yield to others. It is full
of mercy and good deeds. It shows no favoritism and
is always sincere.
JAMES 3:17 NLT

By wisdom a house is built, and by understanding
it is established.
PROVERBS 24:3 NASB